Pan-African Infrastructure Development and Public-Private Partnerships

Vincent J. Napoleon

Contributing Authors

Diana V. Vilmenay-Hammond
Keri A. McWilliams

LexNoir Foundation is the charitable, educational arm of LexNoir, an international network of lawyers connecting the African Diaspora.

This book, *Pan-African Infrastructure Development and Public-Private Partnerships*, is published by LexNoir Foundation and reflects the points of view of the authors and editors as of the date of publication and does not necessarily represent the opinions, interpretations, or positions of the law firms or organizations with which they are affiliated, nor the opinions, interpretations or positions of LexNoir Foundation or LexNoir.

Nothing contained in this book is to be considered as the rendering of legal advice, either generally or in connection with any specific issues or case. Readers are responsible for obtaining advice from their own legal counsel or other professional. This book, any forms and agreements, or other information herein are intended for educational and informational purposes only.

TABLE OF CONTENTS

Page

ABOUT THE AUTHORS

Mr. Vincent Napoleon is a Partner with Nixon Peabody LLP and a member of the firm's Government Contracts team and Commercial Litigation practice group. Mr. Napoleon previously served as general counsel of various business units within Lockheed Martin Corporation and The General Electric Company. Mr. Napoleon is also a retired U.S. Air Force Colonel and formerly the Senior Contracting Official for the Air Force District of Washington and the senior reservist to the Deputy Assistant Secretary of the Air Force (Contracting). He has experience across a wide range of sectors, including transportation, aerospace, federal, state and municipal government facilities, healthcare, life sciences and telecommunications. He represents private sector contractors and the public sector on projects throughout Europe, Asia, Africa, Latin America and Australia.

Mr. Napoleon advises on the full spectrum of infrastructure and public private partnership projects, related to airports, education, energy, health care, highway maintenance, ports, prisons and social justice, railroads, social housing, stadiums and sporting venues. He has led the legal support on large infrastructure projects including the acquisition and financing of the International Terminal of the Philadelphia International Airport (PIA) and the PIA Airport concession in the terminal B/C connector. He has also advised on municipal gas and water projects.

Mr. Napoleon has been engaged in expanding his practice to include sub-Saharan Africa having spent time in cultivating relationships in South Africa, Nigeria, Ghana and other areas of West Africa. Mr. Napoleon received his Juris Doctor (J.D.) from the University of Pittsburgh School of Law in Pittsburgh, Pennsylvania and a Bachelor of Science in Business Administration (B.S.B.A.) with a concentration in International Management and Marketing from Georgetown University in Washington, D.C.

Mr. Napoleon can be contacted at
vnapoleon@nixonpeabody.com

***

Ms. Diana Vilmenay-Hammond is a Department Attorney with Nixon Peabody LLP and a member of the firm's Franchise & Distribution team and Commercial Litigation practice group. She handles domestic and cross-border transactions including licensing and franchising. She has experience across a wide range of sectors, including the transportation sector. She represents clients throughout Europe, Asia, Africa, and Latin America. Ms. Vilmenay practice also includes exposure to franchise-related matters and public-private partnerships in sub-Saharan Africa, Asia, Latin American and the Caribbean. She has written and edited a number of publications regarding public-private partnerships, franchising, mergers and acquisitions and other commercial transactions. Ms. Vilmenay received her Juris Doctor (J.D.) from Howard University School of Law in Washington, D.C. and a Bachelor of Arts (B.A.) in

French and Psychology from Georgetown University in Washington, D.C.

Ms. Vilmenay-Hammond can be contacted at
dvilmenay@nixonpeabody.com

***

Ms. Keri McWilliams is a Senior Associate with Nixon Peabody LLP and a member of the Franchise & Distribution team and Commercial Litigation practice group. Ms. McWilliams regularly counsels franchisors on regulatory compliance and international expansion. Formerly an intern with the Transportation Division of the San Francisco City Attorney's Office, Ms. McWilliams has developed expertise in the use of public private partnerships as an infrastructure development tool. Ms. McWilliams has continued to expand her international practice to include various countries in Africa including South Africa, Nigeria, and Kenya. Ms. McWilliams received her Juris Doctor (J.D.) from Georgetown University Law Center in Washington, D.C. and a Bachelor of Fine Arts from Washington University in St. Louis, in St. Louis, Missouri.

Ms. McWilliams can be contacted at
kmcwilliams@nixonpeabody.com

ACKNOWLEDGMENT

This book could not have been written without the hard work and dedication of each of the contributing authors. I could not have done it without you. Thank you.

I would like to acknowledge and extend my heartfelt gratitude to the Nixon Peabody LLP 2014 Washington, D.C. Summer Associates Nia D. Newton and Katherine M. Hannah, currently students at Georgetown University Law Center, for their invaluable assistance in researching for this publication.

I would also like to acknowledge André Pottas of Deloitte & Touche and Taswell Papier of ENS both in South Africa for their review and editorial comments.

To our family, friends, and others throughout the Nixon Peabody community, words alone cannot express what we owe them for their encouragement that enabled us to complete this work. Kendal, my partner, my colleague, my partner in crime, thank you. A special thanks to my better half, Lisa, for always going the extra mile and providing her invaluable critiques.

FOREWORD

It is an oft-quoted statistic that 6 of the 10 fastest growing economies globally in the past 5 years are in Africa. It is predicted that 7 of the 10 fastest growing economies in the coming 5 years will also be in Africa. Sub-Saharan African growth over the coming decade is forecasted to outstrip that of China. But to achieve and sustain these growth rates of over 6% per annum, and to continue to accelerate this positive economic momentum, it is imperative that investment in infrastructure is accelerated at an even faster rate, with a specific focus on infrastructure that supports manufacturing growth and intra-African trade.

While infrastructure development in Africa has traditionally been financed principally by the fiscus, or by donor agencies, there is a significant shortfall in available funding. This need can only be met by the private sector if Africa is to achieve its anticipated level of infrastructure development resulting from its aggressive short-term growth ambitions.

Public-Private Partnerships provide a proven and efficient means for accessing private capital to deliver, operate and maintain public infrastructure and this model is increasingly being embraced by African governments. Regulatory frameworks are being developed and PPP oversight units are being created in a number of African countries that have not used PPPs before, while those that have experience with this funding mechanism are expanding the number of asset classes where it is being utilized. With support from governments and development finance institutions, and increasing interest from the private sector to participate in these arrangements, there is a bright future for PPPs on the continent.

André Pottas
Infrastructure & Capital Projects Advisory Leader: Africa
Deloitte & Touche

"Economic growth and prosperity depends on modern infrastructure. That much is obvious from a host of developing countries—including those in sub-Saharan Africa, where infrastructure development has accounted for half of the recent acceleration in the region's economic growth…"[1]

Rashad Kaldany
Vice President and Chief Operating Officer
International Finance Corporation

I. INTRODUCTION

Today's global infrastructure demand is estimated at approximately US$4 trillion in annual expenditure.[2] The result is the need for greater investment in infrastructure and a significant supply of private capital from sources such as pension funds, insurance companies, sovereign wealth funds, private equity funds, and other innovative financing and deal structure models. To this end, governments globally are increasingly forging relationships with the private sector for the delivery of services and to support infrastructure development. Recognized as a pillar of growth and prosperity among economies around the world, infrastructure and investment are essential to creating a strong, vibrant and competitive economy. Public-private partnerships (PPPs), for example, are among the many tools governments are using to implement infrastructure development around the world—using the

---

1 World Economic Forum, *Strategic Infrastructure Steps to Prepare and Accelerate Public-Private Partnerships* (May 2013) [hereinafter "Strategic Steps"] at 5.

2 *Id.* at 3.

private sector's financial resources, expertise, business acumen, and technical skills combined with public sector strategic vision to incite innovation in accomplishing infrastructure projects that span sectors from power generation and transportation to water and telecommunications.[3] For example, recognizing the efficacy of PPPs, the U.S. Congress is currently examining how billions of dollars in infrastructure needs could be supported by PPPs as they bring efficiency and discipline to project delivery, which is lacking or sometimes absent in the traditional public procurement process.[4] With a well-defined regulatory environment for PPPs, strong capital markets, a competitive private sector, and a robust economic outlook, South Africa leverages PPPs to not only facilitate infrastructure needs but to also address socioeconomic concerns including job creation, poverty alleviation, and economic growth.[5] With its recently established Public Partnership Act,[6]

---

3 *See* World Economic Forum, *Strategic Infrastructure in Africa: A Business Approach to Project Acceleration* (May 2013) [hereinafter "Strategic Infrastructure"] at 3. The African Union Strategic Plan identifies infrastructure development as a key priority. The resulting "Programme for Infrastructure Development in Africa" was approved by the African heads of state at their summit in Addis Ababa, Ethiopia, in January 2012.

4 Public Private Partnerships: Finding and Recommendations of the Special Panel on Public-Private Partnerships, *Report of the Panel on Public-Private Partnerships to the Committee on Transportation and Infrastructure*, U.S. House of Representatives (September 2014) [hereinafter Transportation and Infrastructure Report], p. 10.

5 Liesel Lombaard, *Public Private Partnerships Enhance Service Delivery*, MAIL & GUARDIAN, November 29, 2012, *available at* http://mg.co.za/article/2012-11-30-00-public-private-partnerships-

(Footnote continued on next page)

Kenya established a legal framework for implementing PPP project delivery as a risk sharing model between the public and private sectors on heavily regulated large projects.[7]

World governments' need for infrastructure investment is driven by a number of factors. For example, by 2050, it is estimated that the global population will increase by approximately 2.3 billion people to approximately 9.3 billion people.[8] By 2050, it is estimated that the urban population worldwide will increase by 2.6 billion people to 6.3 billion.[9] Industrialization and rising living standards in emerging countries will likely drive the global economic growth at a rate of about 2% per year

---

enhance-service-delivery. Also, the law in South Africa defines a PPP as a contract between a public sector institution and a private party, in which the private party assumes a substantial financial, technical, and operational risk in the design, financing, building, and operation of a project. *See* Treasury Regulation 16 issued to the Public Finance Management Act, 1999 (PFMA). PPPs for municipal government are governed by the Municipal Systems Act, 2000, and the Municipal Finance Management Act, 2003. Municipalities are not subject to the PFMA or to Treasury Regulation 16. South Africa has the greatest cumulative experience of PPPs in Africa.

6 *See* the [Kenya] Public Private Partnerships Act, No. 27 of 2013.

7 Rosa Nduati-Mutero, *Public Private Partnerships Act: Regulatory Framework* (May 23, 2013), *available at* http://www.africalegalnetwork.com/wp-content/uploads/2013/05/Regulatory-Regime-PPP-Act-_-Rosa-Nduati-Mutero-_-Dominic-Rebelo.pdf.

8 Strategic Steps, *supra* note 1 at 14.

9 *Id.*

doubling worldwide per capita GDP.[10] The increasing globalization of supply chains and regional economic integration also help drive the need for globally interconnected telecommunications and transportation networks.[11]

Similarly, development of sustainable infrastructure in Africa is intrinsically linked to economic growth resulting from the rising standard of living and increased populations. For example, one of sub-Saharan Africa's top developmental challenges continues to be the shortage of physical infrastructure—inadequate transportation, communication, water, and power infrastructure.[12] This lack of infrastructure has proven to be a major obstacle to growth and development in Africa and has resulted in low level intra-African trade and trade with other regions in the world.[13] This is a view shared by many who are in leadership throughout the African Diaspora. For example, Shamsudeen Usman, Nigeria's Minister of National Planning echoed the sentiment that "infrastructure is a key driver of economic growth and development."[14]

---

10 *Id.*

11 *Id.*

12 André Pottas, *Addressing Africa's Infrastructure Challenges* (Deloitte & Touche, 2012).

13 Irina Unkovski, *Infrastructure Asset Lifecycle: Operational Risk Mitigation From Project Inception*, at 3 (Deloitte & Touche, 2012).

14 Editor, "*Financing Nigeria's Infrastructure: A Case In Favour of Capital Market*," BUSINESSDAY, August 8, 2013, *available at* http://businessdayonline.com/2013/08/financing-nigerias-infrastructure-a-case-in-favour-of-capital-market/#.VDfIXWeYbIU.

Recognizing that the state of infrastructure in Nigeria is inadequate, the minister further concluded that inadequate infrastructure is "a serious constraint to socio-economic development."[15] Indeed, "[i]nfrastructure is the lifeblood of any economy as no economy can grow and develop without a reasonable stock of critical infrastructure in transportation (roads, rail, ports, and airports), energy, water, sanitation, and communication. Where infrastructure is inadequate or ineffective, growth is affected and people's standard of living is negatively impacted."[16]

Accelerating Africa's growth hinges upon addressing infrastructure gaps with projects involving governments using, among other things, the PPP model. This is a view consistent with that which was espoused by President Zuma of South Africa who stated that "[t]he involvement of the private sector is critical to achieving the country's infrastructure initiatives." He emphasized further that "…embark[ing] upon mutually beneficial public-private partnerships in championing [the country's] projects is essential to its future." As such, PPPs as endorsed by President Zuma are fostering dynamism in Africa that is globally acknowledged and is rapidly accelerating Africa's economic growth making it the world's third-fastest growing region.[17]

Africa is embarking on a 20-to-30-year infrastructure development boom.[18] With six of 10 of the

---

15 *Id.*

16 *Id.*

17 Strategic Infrastructure, *supra* note 1 at 6.

18 Pottas, *supra* note 12.

world's most rapidly expanding economies located in sub-Saharan Africa,[19] the efficacy of PPPs as a model leading to the development and improvement of infrastructure and economic growth is self-evident. Indeed, PPPs represent a significant opportunity for investors to engage in the development and financing of ports, railways, toll roads, power stations, hospitals, telecommunications, and other elements of physical infrastructure, which are essential to a 21st century quality of life and essential to sustained growth of a new, modern, and globally competitive Africa.

As a general matter, this paper discusses the PPP project delivery model with the objective of focusing on how this phenomenon of infrastructure procurement finance reform in Africa can have a significant impact on spurring economic development and strengthening economies on the continent. Among other things, this paper will explore Africa as an emerging global player, explain the role of PPPs generally and in Africa and discuss PPPs as they exist in various countries throughout sub-Saharan Africa.

II. AFRICA AS AN EMERGING GLOBAL PLAYER

The Statistics

In recent years, Africa has become a focal point for major market investment. It is the center of some of the world's fastest growing economies positioning the continent as a global economic player. Africa, for example,

---

19 *Id.*

currently has one of the world's fastest growth rates.[20] Between 2011 and 2015, seven of the world's ten fastest-growing economies are forecasted to be African nations.[21] Significant business opportunities comparable to those of the BRIC countries of Brazil, Russia, India, and China continue to emerge from Africa.[22] In about one-third of Africa's 55 countries, annual GDP growth is above 6% while Sub-Saharan Africa grew at an estimated 5.1% pace in 2013.[23] Foreign investors claim that their return on investment in Africa is higher than in any other emerging region.[24] It is also notable that foreign trade partners such as China and India continue to seek out Africa's natural resources.[25]

---

20 Joseph Jimenez, *A Healthier, Wealthier Africa*, THE INDEPENDENT, February 14, 2014, *available at* http://www.independent.co.ug/column/guest-column/8716-a-healthier-wealthier-africa, referring to Africa as a region with the world's second fastest growth.

21 Those countries are Ethiopia, Mozambique, Tanzania, Congo, Ghana, Zambia, and Nigeria. The Economist, *Africa's Impressive Growth*, June 6, 2011, *available at* http://www.economist.com/blogs/dailychart/2011/01/daily_chart. *See also* Howard French, *Seven of the World's 10 Fastest-Growing Economies Are African*, BUSINESS INSIDER, May 21, 2012, *available at* http://www.businessinsider.com/seven-of-the-worlds-10-fastest-growing-economies-are-african-2012-5.

22 Jimenez, *supra*, note 20.

23 *Id.*

24 *Id.*

25 *Id.; See also India Plans to Finance Expansion of Trade and Investment in Africa,* OUT-LAW.COM, March 13, 2014, *available at* http://www.out-law.com/en/articles/2014/march/india-plans-to-finance-expansion-of-trade-and-investment-in-africa/. According to a CII-World Trade Organization Report published last year,

(Footnote continued on next page)

One reason why Africa continues to show such high growth prospects is favorable commodity prices.[26] Indeed, this has benefited oil exporters like Nigeria, Angola and even Ghana.[27] Africa's oil resources are expected to continue to benefit its major exporters according to the BP Energy Outlook 2035.[28] According to this report, twenty years from now, Africa will account for 10% of global oil

---

bilateral India-Africa trade has grown by nearly 32% annually between 2005 and 2011, including through the global economic crisis. The report also states that India-Africa trade is projected to reach US$90bn by 2015.

26 Amadou Sy, *Five Questions Answered on Africa's Rising Economic Growth*, BUSINESS DAY, February 18, 2014, *available at* http://businessdayonline.com/2014/02/five-questions-answered-on-africas-rising-economic-growth/.

27 *Id.* Experts predict varying effects of falling oil and gas prices on Africa. For example, in South Africa the drop in oil prices will likely benefit the country's manufacturers, consumers and transport sectors since they all benefit from lower fuel costs. In East African countries where oil exploration increased, offshore and onshore oil development is expected to decrease while the transportation sector is expected to benefit from lower gas prices. Finally, West Africa is expected to bear the brunt of the impact including potential spending costs and tax increases to offset falling currency. *See* Jeffrey Cavanaugh, Forex Africa: How Will Falling Oil Price Affect Africa's Big-3?, BUSINESS TIMES, January 16, 2015, *available at* http://www.businesstimes.co.tz/index.php?option=com_content&view=article&id=4485:forex-africa-how-will-falling-oil-price-affect-africas-big-3&catid=1:latest-news&Itemid=57.

28 BP Energy Outlook 2035, *available at* http://www.bp.com/content/dam/bp/pdf/Energy-economics/Energy-Outlook/BP_World_Energy_Outlook_booklet_2035.pdf.

and 9% of natural gas production.[29] Wholesale and retail commerce, transportation, telecommunications, and manufacturing are also some of the biggest driving forces on the continent.[30]

Another reason for Africa's developing growth prospects are "medium-term policies" and continued structural reform.[31] Many African countries have embraced democracy and while internal conflicts continue to persist, they have appeared to stabilize more quickly than the major conflicts that dominated international headlines even a decade ago.

Additionally, Africa's longer life expectancy is driving half of the world's future population growth and spurring a burgeoning middle class. This phenomenon may lead to a "demographic dividend" of an adult population of 800 million by 2030 (compared to 460 million in 2010).[32] Africa's rapid urbanization and growing middle class could generate hundreds of millions of consumers.[33] Africa's working-age population is expected to total 1.1 billion people in 2040.[34] By 2030, much of Africa is expected to

---

29 *Id.*

30 French, *supra,* note 21.

31 Sy, *supra*, note *26.*

32 *Id.*

33 *Id.* Notably, Africa currently has more middle class consumers than India, which has a larger population. *See* McKinsey and Company, *Lions on the Move: The progress and potential of African economies*, June 2010. *See also* French, *supra* note 21.

34 If that occurs, it will provide the globe a larger labor force than population-rich China or India. *See* Jimenez, *supra*, note 20.

attain lower-middle to middle class majorities and consumer spending will expand from US$680 billion in 2008 to US$2.2 trillion.[35] In addition, by 2030 it is anticipated that 50% of Africans will live in cities.[36]

Over the next several years, Africa's consumer market is expected to be worth US$1 trillion.[37] The market will be driven by consumer demands for technological goods such as vehicles, cellphones, and household appliances.[38] These expectations suggest that Africans are willing to spend just as much or even more than Europeans, Americans, and Japanese consumers on technology.[39] While these statistics are impressive, it is important to note that they are relative. For example, Africans generally spend more on goods primarily due to import costs.[40]

---

35 French, *supra,* note 21.

36 Standard Bank, The Five Trends Powering Africa's Enduring Allure, Trend 2: Africa's Transformational Urban Swell, September 21, 2011, *available at* http://www.standardbank.com/Africa%20Macro_5%20trends%20powering%20Africa's%20allure%20(Trend%202-Urbanisation)%20(2).pdf.

37 Sulaiman Philip, *Middle Class Africa: Meet the New African Consumer*, BIZCOMMUNITY.COM, February 21, 2014, *available at* http://www.bizcommunity.com/Article/410/87/110001.html.

38 *Id.* It is expected that the South African electronics market alone will be worth around US$13-billion by 2016.

39 *Id.*

40 *Id.* This is one of the major challenges that face some companies trying to tap into the market place. The demand for competitively priced technology has led to the growth of companies willing to offer them. Middle Eastern computer companies have been able to carve out market share for themselves as suppliers of low-cost

(Footnote continued on next page)

New Opportunities for Africa

To accommodate Africa's burgeoning growth, the African Union Strategic Plan, developed in May 2013, outlines the African Union's main priorities for economic development over the next four years. It specifically identifies infrastructure development in sectors such as energy, power generation and distribution, transportation, water, and telecommunications as a crucial priority.[41] These development plans may translate to almost US$70 billion in capital expenditures by 2020. In fact, some research estimates that infrastructure development in Africa must exceed US$1 trillion per year for the next seven years to stay on course with global demands.[42] The expected growth creates the potential for new opportunities for international private sector investment.

Country-by-country, Africa infrastructure development is a critical priority and the key to substantial economic growth. For example, with infrastructure development as a basis, the International Monetary Fund

---

computer equipment. The performance of companies like Huawei, Nokia, and Blackberry has outstripped Apple because their handsets are far more affordable. Another factor in the choices made by the emerging middle class of one brand over another is a product's suitability to African conditions. *Id.*

41 *See* Press Release, African Union Commission's Strategic Plan 2014–2017 adopted by Assembly.

42 According to the World Bank, this estimate is for developing economies. Another US$200–$300 billion is needed to ensure that infrastructure is low emitting and climate resilient. World Bank, IFC and World Economic Forum, *Tackling the Infrastructure Finance Deficit*, January 2013.

(IMF) concluded that Nigeria's economy would grow by 7.3% in 2014, up from 6.4% in 2013.[43] Multiple Nigerian sectors other than energy are expected to drive the growth, with inflation on the decline and a further reduction in 2014.[44] At the end of the year, inflation will be 7%, a reduction of 0.9% from last year's 7.9%, continuing a two-year downslope, which has been encouraged by the country's tight monetary policy.[45] Economic growth is expected to improve further in 2014, driven by agriculture, trade, and services with the expectation that inflation will continue to decline.[46]

As another example, Kenya has received five-year funding of Sh79.2 billion (US$915 million) from the African Development Bank (AfDB) to boost economic empowerment, infrastructure upgrades and job creation.[47] According to the AfDB, the funds, which would be made available from 2014–2018, will be spent on infrastructure development and tertiary education.[48] The AfDB has

---

43 Editor, IMF Predicts 7.3% Economic Growth For Nigeria in 2014, VENTURES AFRICA, March 9, 2014, *available at* http://www.ventures-africa.com/2014/03/imf-predicts-7-3-economic-growth-for-nigeria-in-2014/.

44 *Id.*

45 *Id.*

46 *Id.*

47 Editor, Kenya Receives US$915m from AfDB to Fund Economic Development, VENTURES AFRICA, March 7, 2014, *available at* http://www.ventures-africa.com/2014/03/kenya-receives-915m-from-afdb-to-fund-economic-development/.

48 *Id.*

indicated that it will continue to support the Kenyan government's effort to improve infrastructure as a means of unlocking inclusive growth and developing skills for the country's emerging labor market.[49] AfDB has noted that its focus is on infrastructural development such as water, energy, and roads, since it believes such development will increase the population's access to basic utilities.[50]

Potential Barriers to True Economic Growth

While Africa's economic growth has made the continent attractive to private investment, there continues to be concerns regarding structural obstacles to infrastructure development.[51] These concerns include a lack of clear legislation and enforcement of commercial law in some countries, a low degree of transparency in the procurement process, and a mixed track record in implementing PPPs.[52]

Therefore, Africa's strides to become a truly global player are not without challenges. The AfDB has emphasized that Africa must improve investment in industrialization and trade facilitation to guarantee that the growth momentum that many countries are currently experiencing is more "resilient to external shocks and translates into economic transformation."[53] Unemployment,

---

49 *Id.*

50 *Id.*

51 *Id.* at 3, p.11.

52 *Id.*

53 African Bank Development Group, *Industrialization A Precondition for Africa's Economic Transformation*, October 30, 2013, *available at* http://www.afdb.org/en/news-and-

(Footnote continued on next page)

disease, violence and the staggering poverty rate of many African countries are major barriers to sustained growth in Africa.[54] Additionally, the AfDB has expressed its concerns to African governments about increased political stability due to high rates of unemployment of African youths.[55]

While Africa has experienced economic success due to factors such as a vibrant export market, these factors have not necessarily contributed to job creation, which is a major component of true economic growth. What has been cited as the "paradox of Africa's growth" can be attributed to a number of factors.[56] As noted, one reason is that exports of commodities and natural resources have been the

---

events/article/industrialization-a-precondition-for-africas-economic-transformation-12466/

54 Africa's economic growth has not yet translated into millions of wage-paying jobs. Obadias Ndaba, *The Paradox of Africa's Growth*, THE HUFFINGTON POST, February 14, 2014, *available at* http://www.huffingtonpost.com/obadias-ndaba/the-paradox-of-africas-gr_b_4741067.html. The Ebola outbreak and ongoing violence by religious insurgents has also challenged various regions. For example, while it may have a lingering impact on countries directly affected by the Ebola virus (e.g. Liberia, Sierra Leone and Guinea), for the most part the economic impact on most African economies will be less than previously forecasted. *See, e.g.* Press Release, Ebola: Most African Countries Avoid Major Economic Loss but Impact on Guinea, Liberia, Sierra Leone Remains Crippling (Jan. 20, 2015) *available at* http://www.worldbank.org/en/news/press-release/2015/01/20/ebola-most-african-countries-avoid-major-economic-loss-but-impact-on-guinea-liberia-sierra-leone-remains-crippling.

55 *Id.*

56 *Id.*

driving force of Africa's economic growth.[57] While commodities exports help increase government coffers (i.e., oil exports) they do not require a huge labor force.[58] Another reason is that African governments lose money through "illicit financial outflows" such as corruption, tax evasion, and bribes.[59] According to a 2013 study by the AfDB and Global Financial Integrity, a nonprofit research and advocacy organization, Africa lost over US$1 trillion dollars to corruption, tax evasion, and bribes from 1980 to 2009.[60] Of the top 25 countries with the highest measured cumulative illicit financial outflows between 2002 and 2011, Nigeria and South Africa were both listed.[61] A recent article notes:

> This amount is more than three times the total amount of foreign aid received in the same period and twenty-eight times higher than the annual foreign direct investments to Africa which, according to the United Nations Conference on Trade and Development, was at 50 billion in 2012. If this trend was reversed,

57 *Id.*

58 *Id.*

59 *Id.*

60 *Id.*

61 Global Financial Integrity Chart, Top 25 Countries With Highest Measured Cumulative Illicit Financial Outflows Between 2002 and 2011, *available at* http://www.gfintegrity.org/report/2013-global-report-illicit-financial-flows-from-developing-countries-2002-2011/.

> Africa would be able to solve all of its economic woes with no outside assistance.[62]

Tax systems that fail to redistribute wealth and disadvantage the poor have also been blamed. For example in various sub-Saharan countries, natural resource mining is a sector "known to be rife with tax-dodging techniques."[63] Another reason is that manufacturing contributes less than it should to Africa's GDP and to the labor market.[64] In East Africa, the lack of infrastructure development both intra-province and inter-province has also been cited as a culprit for disparities in growth across all sectors of society.[65]

The definition of "middle class" is also relative. According to the AfDB, the African middle class comprises people that spend between US$2 and US$20 a day.[66] Approximately 60% of Africa's middle class spend US$2-

---

62 Ndaba, *supra* note 48.

63 Katie Allen, *Poor Losing Out In African Boom According to New Report*, THE GUARDIAN, February 23, 2014, *available at* http://www.theguardian.com/world/2014/feb/24/poor-losing-out-african-boom.

64 Ndaba, *supra* note 48.

65 Michael Meyer, *East Africa's Prosperity Gap*, PROJECT SYNDICATE, March 5, 2014, *available at* http://www.project-syndicate.org/commentary/michael-meyer-points-out-that-the-region-s-rapid-economic-growth-is-overwhelmingly-benefiting-the-very-rich.

66 Alex O Awiti, *The Myth, Reality of Kenya Middle Class*, THE STAR, March 4, 2014, *available at* http://www.the-star.co.ke/news/article-157626/myth-reality-kenya-middle-class.

US$4 per day, subsisting just above the regional poverty line.[67] Most of this middle class works in the informal sector, a part of the economy that is generally not taxed, monitored, or included in the gross national product (GNP). On the one hand, this middle class segment is vulnerable to shocks and can easily slide into poverty depending on the circumstances.[68] On the other hand, the more stable middle class spends more than US$4 a day and includes about 128 million Africans as of 2010.[69] As a result, increased investment in employment-generating sectors and industries is critical such that the paradox of Africa's growth does not become an eternal reality.[70]

As discussed in the next section, PPPs are a potential catalyst for increased infrastructure development, economic growth, and job creation on the continent.

III. PUBLIC-PRIVATE PARTNERSHIPS

The term public-private partnership describes a variety of arrangements that involve the public sector working in tandem with the private sector.[71] There are two

---

67 *Id.*

68 *Id.*

69 *Id.*

70 *Id.*

71 The following overview was obtained from a number of sources including: The World Bank, ICA, PPIAF, Project Preparation Guide to African Public-Private Partnerships: A Project Preparation Guide (2009)[hereinafter Project Preparation Guide]; Vincent J. Napoleon and Diana Vilmenay, *Investors: Prepare Now to Take Advantage of African Public-Private Partnerships in*

(Footnote continued on next page)

important characteristics of PPPs—investment by the private sector and significant risk transfer from the public sector to the private sector.[72] While this model for delivering infrastructure projects across the world has been gaining traction among the public sector as a way to close the infrastructure gap, PPPs have been increasing rapidly in emerging and developing countries.[73]

PPPs have been used as a means to implement infrastructure development across the globe. PPPs facilitate and provide required infrastructure assets in instances where governments lack the full financial resources and expertise.[74] In such cases, governments look to the private sector to assist in accelerating development.[75] In this specific context, PPP describes the relationship where the private sector provides public infrastructure under a long-term contract with a public authority such as a local government or agency. These PPP projects are typically

---

2014, Nixon Peabody Alert, December 17, 2013, *available at* http://www.nixonpeabody.com/investors_prepare_to_take_advantage_of_PPP_in_2014 [hereinafter Napoleon] and Vincent J. Napoleon and Diana Vilmenay, Pan-African Infrastructure Development Means Future Investment Opportunities and New Public-Private Partnerships, Nixon Peabody Alert, November 12, 2013, *available at* http://www.nixonpeabody.com/Pan_African_infrastructure_development [hereinafter Napoleon 2].

72 Teresa Ter-Minassian, International Monetary Fund, Public-Private Partnerships at 6 (March 12, 2004).

73 Strategic Steps, *supra*, note 1 at 16.

74 *Id.* at 7-8.

75 *Id.*

large endeavors that bring capital to the market and create local job opportunities, which in turn, when effective, spur consumption, increase wealth and promote stronger economies.[76] "In certain circumstances, [PPPs] can bring innovative solutions to infrastructure challenges....a broad array of interested and invested parties...substantial [project] experience... [financial rigor and incentive from the private sector] to deliver project[s] on-time and on-budget."[77] PPP projects also tend to draw other private investors to the market, thus creating a stronger model for long-term economic growth.[78]

To understand PPPs is to envision a project delivery model that exists somewhere between public project delivery and privatization.

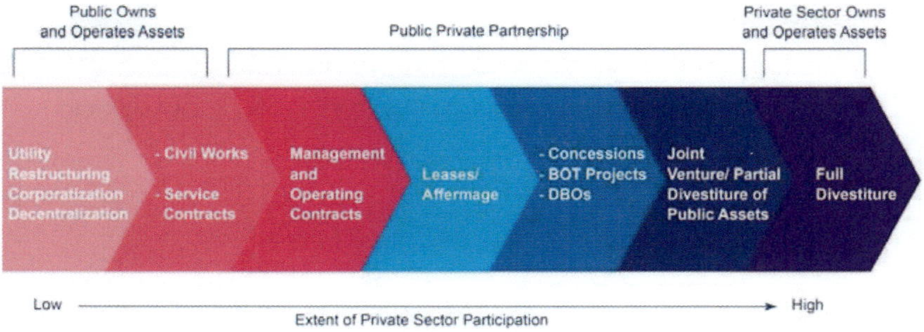

Figure 1
Source: http://ppp.worldbank.org/public-private-partnership/agreements

[76] Napoleon 2, *supra*, note 71.

[77] Transportation and Infrastructure Report, *supra* note 4 at 10.

[78] Napoleon 2, *supra*, note 71.

There are many different types of PPPs. However, for discussion purposes, the focus is on a public-private partnership that allows a private party to provide a public infrastructure under a long-term contract with a government agency or other type of public sector agency.[79] Under such a relationship the private party would likely agree to "design, build or upgrade the [infrastructure], assume substantial financial, technical and operational risks, [has some control over the asset, raise private finance for capital expenditures], receive a financial return through payments over the life of the contract from users, from the public sector, or from a combination of the two, [and, if applicable], return the infrastructure to public sector ownership at the end of the contract."[80]

Ultimately, the PPP is "determined by what rights, obligations, and risks are assumed by the public or private parties within the partnership."[81] There are three main forms of PPPs: concession, build-operate transfer (BOT), and design-build-operate (DBO).[82] The decision to use any one of the three forms or any variant thereof (*See* Figure 2 below for variations of PPP schemes) is based on policy and business considerations.[83] For example, some of the policy and business questions that should be considered are:

---

79 Project Preparation Guide, *supra* note 71 at 8.

80 *Id.*

81 *Id.*

82 *Id.*

83 *Id.* at 10.

- How should a reasonable rate of return be established?
- How should the term of the PPP agreement be determined?
- How should the public sector evaluate the trade-off between upfront payments and the ability to share in revenues over the term?
- How should upfront or annual proceeds of a transaction be spent?
- Can the public sector achieve the same or better financial results as a PPP through public borrowings and public operation?
- How can the quality of long-term maintenance be assured?
- How to ensure that a leased facility will be returned to the public sector at the end of the term in a state of good repair?
- What criteria should be used to select appropriate projects for PPPs?
- How can competition be assured, and the procurement process be made fair and transparent?

- How can the public sector be protected in the event of the private partner's default or bankruptcy?

- How do PPPs impact existing employees in concessions of existing assets?[84]

[84] These questions for consideration may be found in their original format in the United States Department of Transportation Federal Highway Administration, *Public Policy Considerations in Public-Private Partnership (PPP) Arrangements* (January 2009).

PPP Schemes and Modalities

Schemes	**Modalities**
Build-own-operate (BOO) Build-develop-operate (BDO) Design-construct-manage-finance (DCMF)	The private sector designs, builds, owns, develops, operates and manages an asset with no obligation to transfer ownership to the government. These are variants of design-build-finance-operate (DBFO) schemes.
Buy-build operate (BBO) Lease-develop-operate (LDO) Wrap-around addition (WAA)	The private sector buys or leases an existing asset from the government, renovates, modernizes, and/or expands it, and then operates the asset, again with no obligation to transfer ownership back to the government.
Build-operate-transfer (BOT) Build-own-operate-transfer (BOOT) Build-rent-own-transfer (BROT) Build-lease-operate-transfer (BLOT) Build-transfer-operate (BTO)	The private sector designs and builds and asset, operates it, and then transfers it to the government when the operating contract ends, or at some other pre-specified time. The private partner may subsequently rent or lease the asset from the government.

Figure 2
Source: International Monetary Fund, Public-Private Partnership (March 12, 2004) at 8.

Concession

In a concession PPP, a public authority grants a private operator responsibility for the operation, maintenance, financing, and management of an infrastructure asset while the authority retains ownership of the asset and receives all rights to the asset once the concession has ended.[85] Notably, under a concession, the operator assumes the risk for the condition of the asset and for the investment itself.[86] A concession PPP can be provided for an existing asset or utility or for a new build project.[87] The concession period typically lasts from approximately 25–30 years. The public pays for the use of the concession and these payments operate as the source of revenue for the operator.[88] One unique aspect of the concession is that the asset provides instant cash flow to pay the operator and to set aside funds to pay back the investment and/or to service debt. Another unique aspect of the concession is the focus on output as opposed to input.[89] For concessions, the operator will generally set the parameters for operation of the asset and performance standards.

Build-Operate Transfer

In a BOT project, the public authority grants to a private company the right to develop and operate, for a certain period, a facility or system that is traditionally a

---

85 World Bank, PPP in Infrastructure Resource Center, *available a*t http://ppp.worldbank.org/public-private-partnership/agreements/concessions-bots-dbos.

86 *Id.*

87 *Id.*

88 *Id.*

89 *Id.*

public sector project. Under this scenario, the operator would finance, own, and construct the facility or system and then operate it commercially for a concession period. After the concession period is over, the facility is transferred to the public authority. One unique aspect of the BOT is that it is a "classic tool for project finance."[90] For example, the revenues are often obtained from a single "offtake purchaser" such as a utility or government, who purchases project output from the project company.[91] Unlike the concession PPP, there is no instant revenue stream from the facility or system and the operator usually serves as a special purpose vehicle.

Design-Build-Operate

In a DBO the public sector owns and finances the construction of new assets. The private sector designs, builds, and operates the assets to meet certain agreed outputs. The documentation for a DBO is typically simpler than a BOT or Concession as there are no financing documents and will typically consist of a civil works contract plus an operating contract, or a section added to the contract covering operations. The Operator is taking no financing risk and will typically be paid a sum for the design-build of the plant and then an operating fee for the operating period.[92]

---

90 *Id.*

91 *Id.*

92 *Id.*

IV. ADVANTAGES AND CHALLENGES OF PUBLIC-PRIVATE PARTNERSHIP

PPPs offer various potential advantages. One significant advantage of PPPs is there flexibility. More specifically, PPPs offer public sector decision makers an opportunity to improve the delivery of services and the management of facilities. PPPs also help to mobilize private capital, which ultimately facilitates the development and accelerates the delivery of public infrastructure.[93] Use of the PPP project delivery model may also result in filtering out economically underproductive projects. PPPs may also result in reducing the delay in project implementation and the investment in technologies and process innovations, which may reduce project life-cycle costs.[94]

By improving the identification of a project's long-term risks and the allocation of those risks between the public and private sectors, the PPP process enables a more efficient use of resources. Having a PPP contract in place acts as an incentive to both parties to ensure that the infrastructure asset is protected and maintained in the long-term. In short, the public sector can no longer procure infrastructure assets if it fails to adequately maintain them properly. The private sector, on the other hand, has capital invested in these projects. Therefore, it is in the private sector's best interest to design, build, and/or operate these assets taking into account the costs of longer-term maintenance and renewal.

---

93 Strategic Infrastructure, *supra*, note 3 at 7-9.

94 *Id.* at 8.

V. THE AFRICAN PUBLIC-PRIVATE PARTNERSHIP

Currently, the types of infrastructure development that are vital to regional growth in Africa are in areas such as transportation, energy, telecom, and water. Research shows that strengthening these infrastructures is directly linked to a developing nation's ability to sustain a better standard of living and to increase its global trade partners. Additionally, the research of various development banks indicates that the rate of a country's GDP growth is directly linked to the increasing number of PPP projects launched in the country.[95] For example, a World Bank report notes that countries with over 70 PPP infrastructure projects had a 25% GDP growth rate between 1990 and 2003.[96]

---

[95] Booz & Co., *Public-Private Partnerships: A New Catalyst for Economic Growth* (2008), *available at* http://www.strategyand.pwc.com/media/uploads/Public-Private-Partnerships.pdf.

[96] Zambia Development Agency, *Public-Private Partnerships in Infrastructure Development in Zambia* (Jan. 29, 2014) *available at* http://www.zda.org.zm/sites/default/files/Public-Private%20Partnership%20in%20Infrastructure%20Development%20in%20Zambia.pdf.

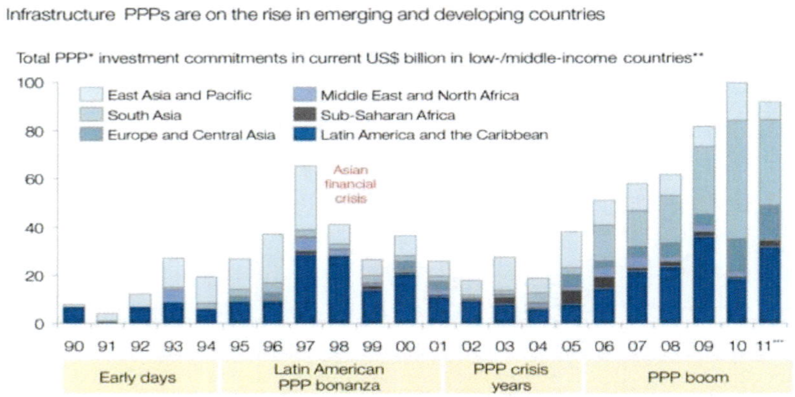

* This includes management and lease contracts, concessions (or management & operation contracts with major private capital commitments), and greenfield projects (excl. merchant contracts), but excludes divestitures/privatizations. ** Following the World Bank definition *** Data as of December 2012. Sometimes projects are included in the database later, hence 2011 figures may be downward biased.

Figure 3

Source: Strategic Steps, *supra* note 1 at 17; *see also* The World Bank and Public-Private Infrastructure Advisory Facility (PPIAF), Private Participation in Infrastructure Database, 2012, *available at* http://ppi.worldbank.org/index.aspx.

According to the African Infrastructure Country Diagnostic (AICD), the continent's infrastructure spending needs stands at about US$93 billion per year.[97] The local governments of many African countries lack the budget power to support these large-scale infrastructure projects on

97 *See also* Daniel Lubogo, *Public Private Partnerships: The Chain Link to Developing East Africa*, The New Vision, *available at* http://www.newvision.co.ug/mobile/Detail.aspx?NewsID=648675&CatID=4. The World Bank estimates that just the maintenance of infrastructure projects in developing countries may cost approximately US$849 million or more.

their own. Therefore, the support of the private sector is vital because the private sector supplies the money, technology, and know-how necessary to launch the PPP projects.

Private investors interested in PPPs are concerned about financial risk and the rate of return on their investments. To address these concerns, groups like the Southern African Development Community (SADC) Public-Private Partnership Network, the New Partnership for Africa's Development (NEPAD) Business Foundation, and development banks like the AfDB, are working with local African governments to help create attractive incentives for private investment. This involves advising governments on policy and institutional reform including encouraging governments to establish and enforce anti-corruption policies, to create transparent PPP legislation, to encourage rate and monetary stability and to lower business transaction costs. These groups are also working with larger agencies to create standard PPP documentation and procedures and to conduct feasibility studies. Finally, these groups are looking at creative ways for private investors to gain significant returns on their investments through long-term equity investments and other revenue produced by the infrastructure, such as toll roads.

Indeed, various regional groups in Africa are working to promote PPP development on the continent on a much larger scale including, through the following means. For example, last year, the SADC PPP Network and NEPAD convened in Johannesburg, South Africa, to launch the first public-private partnership forum geared specifically towards infrastructure development in SADC's fifteen member states.[98] The forum's goal was to set in motion SADC's master plan for investments of US$500 billion in infrastructure development between 2014 and 2027.[99] Specifically, SADC's master plan calls for US$100 billion in international private sector dollars and the participation of PPPs in a number of regional infrastructure projects.[100] Other examples of regional coordination to promote PPP development on the continent include:

- In June 2013, Transnet SOC Ltd. and NEPAD started the Africa Infrastructure Desk, a platform to link the public and private sector on transactions across Africa;[101]

---

98 The member states are Angola, Botswana, Democratic Republic of Congo, Lesotho, Madagascar, Malawi, Mauritius, Mozambique, Namibia, Seychelles, South Africa, Swaziland, United Republic of Tanzania, Zambia and Zimbabwe.

99 Joseph Ngwawi, *2013 Year of Regional Development*, Southern Africa Today (February 23, 2013).

100 SADC, Regional Infrastructure Development Master Plan (2012), *available at* http://webcache.googleusercontent.com/search?q=cache:hJrz8auq98IJ:www.sadc.int/files/7513/5293/3530/Regional_Infrastructure_Development_Master_Plan_Executive_Summary.pdf+&cd=2&hl=en&ct=clnk&gl=us.

101 Press Release, Transnet and the NEPAD Business Foundation launch the Africa Infrastructure Desk (June 2013) (*available at* http://nepadbusinessfoundation.org/index.php/news/latest-news/241-transnet-and-the-nepad-business-foundation-launch-the-africa-infrastructure-desk).

- In May 2013, SADC PPP Network tasked global consultant firm KPMG to study the main objectives of SADC's master plan and short-term action plan (which was launched at SADC's summit in Angola in August 2012) to encourage cooperation among SADC member states in assessing and implementing infrastructure projects in a number of sectors including energy, transport, technology, and tourism;[102]

- In November 2012, at the 4th Annual Public Private Partnership Conference in Abuja, Nigeria, the AfDB confirmed its role as a backer of future PPP projects providing comfort to governments and professionals that PPPs are a long-term strategy for development in Africa;

- The Development Bank of Southern Africa, which is wholly owned by the South African government, has financed and advised on infrastructure funding and disbursed billions of U.S. dollars on infrastructure development; and

- In December 2013, Johannesburg, South Africa, hosted the 5th Annual Public Private Partnership Conference. Primary objectives of the conference were to provide a platform

[102] Mark Allix, *Infrastructure PPP Forum Launched to Boost Regional Development*, Business Day Live (October 24, 2013).

> to demonstrate that PPPs are commercially viable and to serve as a unique platform to discuss ways of mobilizing PPPs to develop much-needed infrastructure in Africa.

African leaders have noted that interest continues to grow in infrastructure development in Africa, particularly with big multinational companies. These companies see the many benefits of their participation in PPP s including projects that will result in narrowing of the infrastructure gap, addressing socioeconomic issues, and creating opportunities for job growth while improving their profits and efficiency in doing business in Africa. In addition to private sector benefits resulting from PPP projects, the public sector also sees significant benefits. Notably, with financing being spurred by the private sector, the public sector gains the ability to engage in large and significant projects on a typically off-balance sheet basis.

VI. FINANCING

Project funding is a critical component of sustained infrastructure development. Traditional sources of funding for infrastructure projects such as annual government budget allocations, multilateral financing, and international grants are generally inadequate to bridge the gap between available funds and monies required to develop and implement the infrastructures necessary to transform Africa into a larger global economic player.[103] As noted earlier, the AICD estimates financing needs for infrastructure development in Africa are estimated to be in excess of

[103] Napoleon, *supra* note 71.

US$93 billion per year.[104] Just under half of the US$93 billion (approximately US$45 billion per year) is currently financed by a combination of funds from multilateral and bilateral resources yielding an infrastructure financing gap of US$45 billion with an infrastructure financing gap of approximately US$48 billion.[105]

PPPs, as an infrastructure project delivery model, are currently the primary financing vehicle and structure used by official development assistance and private sector sources. As a result, infrastructure development projects in Africa facilitated by PPPs create a financially-beneficial opportunity for private investors to help tackle societal improvements. Investors can be better positioned to answer the call for the need of infrastructure development with their keen understanding of the PPP structures and financing models, as they are evolving on the continent.

Financing Models

One of the major components of a PPP arrangement is financing. There are a number of models available for financing PPP infrastructure projects. For example, one financing model is government funding. Government funding is typically used in DBO projects where a government or public authority will source projects through traditional procurement methods and contract with a private company to design, build, operate, and maintain the asset.

---

[104] *See* footnote 97. Strategic Infrastructure, *supra* note 3 at 9; *see also* Mark Pearson, *Financing Infrastructure Through Innovative Strategies in Africa*, Great Insights (May/June 2013).

[105] *Id.*

Documentation for this arrangement is centered on a contract between the sponsoring public authority and the private company. In addition, the parties engage in the consummation of an operating agreement with the private company, which assumes little to no risk.[106]

Another financing model used in the PPP process is Corporate or On-Balance Sheet financing.[107] Utilizing this model, financing is generally obtained by the private company based on its balance sheet versus the project itself.[108] This financing model is typically used in lower value projects.

The most widely used of the financing models in PPP projects is Project Finance.[109] Project Finance is the result of direct investment by private sector investors utilizing the capital markets or limited recourse lending to a specially created project vehicle to support infrastructure projects.[110]

---

106 *See* discussion above regarding DBO model at page 11.

107 Public-Private Partnership in Infrastructure Resource Center, *Main Financing Mechanisms for Infrastructure Projects* [hereinafter Main Financing Mechanisms], *available at* http://ppp.worldbank.org/public-private-partnership/financing/mechanisms (last accessed Oct. 9, 2014).

108 *Id.*

109 *Id.*

110 *Id.*

Financing Structure

Generally, the project sponsors and investors will establish a specially created project vehicle or a special purpose vehicle (SPV) to sign the PPP contract with the government entity and act as the borrower for project capital. The SPV is usually established as a separate legal entity to diminish liability for any parent company.[111] Establishing the SPV as a distinct entity also allows the SPV to finance large projects separate and apart from its parent's balance sheets.[112] As indicated in Figure 4 below, the SPV is the center of the PPP venture, serving as the go-between for the public authority, the actual contractors, and ultimate operators of the project.

111 *Id.*

112 Napoleon, *supra*, note 71.

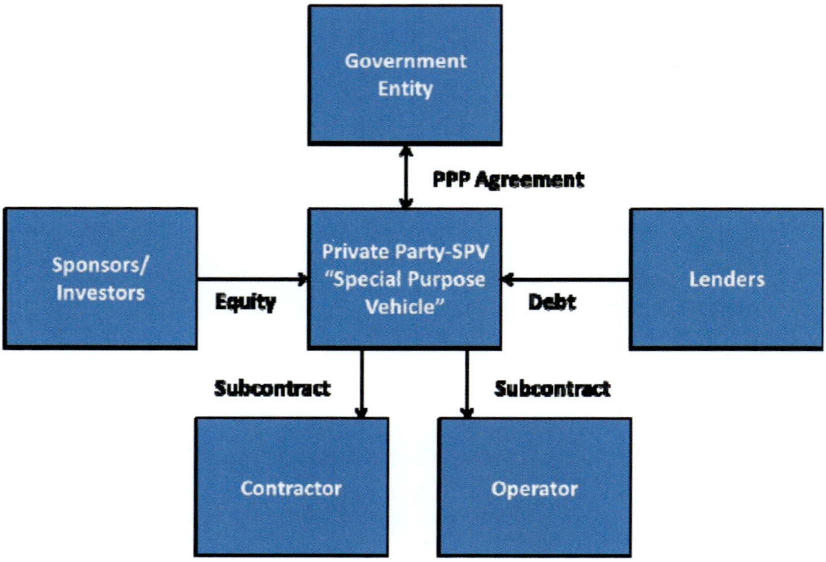

Figure 4
Source: Author. *See also* Project Preparation Guide, *supra* note 71 at 28.

Ultimately, a PPP's financing structure will depend on risk assessment, affordability limits, and the "bankability" of the underlying venture.[113] This is important considering that even for just initial project preparation, costs can range from US$3 million to US$10 million depending on the project.[114] Infrastructure projects in particular have large up-front capital costs during the preparation and construction phases followed by typically smaller operational costs.

[113] Main Financing Mechanisms, *supra* note 107.

[114] Project Preparation Guide, *supra* note 71 at 41.

While the financing structure of a PPP depends on the specific project, industry and available funding sources for each project, PPP projects are typically financed in a similar fashion to project finance arrangements. In these arrangements, lenders and investors use non-recourse financing or limited recourse financing, which are reliant on cash flow generated by the project to repay debts and earn returns for investors. Indeed, a lender's primary assessment to determine risk is the cash flow an infrastructure project is likely to generate in its lifetime of operation and, more specially, the cash flow that is left after operating costs have been paid.[115] For this reason, the terms of the underlying PPP contract are vital to securing financing.

Generally, the private sector investor in the project will raise debt and equity in order to finance the PPP venture. Many PPP projects are funded with a mix of long-term debt finance and equity financing. "Senior debt" is the top-tier funding that lenders may provide to a project. "Mezzanine debt" or "junior debt" may also be part of the PPP financing package. Senior debt has priority for repayment followed by mezzanine debt. Debt financing is primarily used because it is generally less risky than equity financing. Lenders typically require equity funding for PPP

115 This is referred to as a project's bankability. A project is bankable when lenders are willing to finance the project. Banks will look to the cash flow of a project as the primary source of security for the loan. This is quite different from corporate financing the more usual basis on which banks lend to businesses where lenders rely on the value of the company's assets. *See* the EPEC PPP Guide, *available at* eib.org/epec/g2g/i-project-identification/12/123/index.

deals to bridge the gap between the available monies and those monies required to pay the debt. Consequently, investors and the primary contractors will generally provide the equity financing. Similar to debt financing, the returns will depend on project performance.

However, since returns on equity are received after the debt is paid off, equity funding is more risky but can also yield higher returns. In some instances, the government may help provide capital for the initial costs of the project through grants or other means.[116]

If the project's cash flow does not match the debt financing, the difference must typically be covered by a government guarantee.[117] The International Bank for Reconstruction and Development notes that since it can be harder to exercise these alternate options for African PPP projects, PPP project funders, such as traditional lenders, will assess up front whether the long-term funding matches the currency of the project revenue.[118] Other projects consist of funding through varying combinations of private equity, corporate financing, government funding, bonds, and private capital inflows or other unique sources. In Africa, for example, development finance institutions (DFIs), such as the World Bank, the African Development Bank (AfDB), and the Development Bank of Southern Africa, are critical lenders. These DFIs contribute 36% of

---

116 Project Preparation Guide, *supra*, note 71 at 26.

117 *Id.*

118 *Id.*

all funding on the continent, therefore making DFIs the largest funders.[119]

Sources of Financing

Generally, long-term debt finance makes up most of the third-party funding for PPP projects. According to research, long-term debt finance typically ranges from 70 percent to 90 percent of the total funding required depending on each project's perceived risks.[120] Since debt financing tends to carry less risk than equity financing, it is a cheaper funding source.

In addition to debt financing, there are a number of innovative financing instruments utilized in African project finance to support the PPP infrastructure projects. For example, the use of infrastructure bonds, project facilities, equity, and guarantees are just a few of the financing sources that are used to facilitate a PPP and therefore stimulate economic growth in the project country. A type and source of financing utilized in the PPP infrastructure project is dependent upon the phase of the project cycle for which financing is required. *(See* Figure 5 for the type of financing typically required at each stage of the project cycle).

119 *See* Deloitte & Touche African Construction Trends Report 2013.

120 Project Preparation Guide, *supra* note 71 at 25.

Project Cycle	Risk Features	Finance	Providers (include)
Development	The development phase takes the project from the idea stage to bankability. The main risk is that funds are used for feasibility, legal services, technical design and other activities, but that the project does not go ahead.	**Sponsor/ Developer Equity**	InfraCo Africa, Infra Ventures, AFC, Transcentury, IPS, Transcorp, Aldwych, Globeleq, Sithe Global, Agua Imara, Tata, Sino Hydro, Biotherm, Sybion, Aeolus, Amaya, Cluff Geothermal, Ormat, Kenergy and AER Other operators such as utilities, telecom operators and port operators (Maersk, Hutchison, etc.)
		Bridge Financing	Limited instances of banks/DFIs providing bridge loans
Construction	The risk of completing a project on time and within budget is significant, even for well understood technologies. Cost overruns or start-up delays can quickly erode the economic performance of a project, including preventing it from meeting its debt-service obligations. Lenders require construction to be either carried out by a reputable EPC contractor at a fixed-price, time certain basis, or be guaranteed.	**Construction Equity**	Developers/operators also provide construction equity Funds: PAIDF, AIIF, SSIF Development Finance Institutions (selected) Construction firms such as Oderbrecht, Oracom
		Construction Debt	DFIs, plus debt funds (EAIF and the ICF Debt Pool) Export Credit Agencies and Export-Import Banks African and international banks Some pension funds such as Old Mutual
Completion	Once a project is complete it is largely de-risked. However, aspects of project economics are still unknown, including uncontrollable operating costs and market demand.	**Secondary**	Debt can be refinanced in international or local loan or bond markets, depending on market appetite and conditions. Bank portfolios can be aggregated, such as South African banks' book of renewable IPP projects.
Operation	Revenues and costs become better known once a project is commercially operational. The operational performance of a company against contractual/commercial targets becomes the main risk. Lenders derive comfort from the experience of the operator in managing performance.	**- Equity - Debt**	Debt can be refinanced in international or local loan or bond markets; depending on market appetite and conditions. Bank portfolios can be aggregated, such as South African banks' book of renewable IPP projects.

Figure 5

Source: Strategic Infrastructure, *supra* note 3 at 7.

The infrastructure or project bond is an instrument that is receiving more attention especially in the African context.[121] This is especially meaningful given that the credit profiles of African countries have improved in response to high GDP growth rates.[122] When issued, these instruments raise capital for projects, are repaid from money the project generates, and are subject to certain risks specific to the project.[123] With the growing investor base more open to African credits than previously, these instruments may play a significant role in closing the infrastructure funding gap. Pioneering the use of infrastructure bonds in Africa, Kenya has successfully issued infrastructure bonds to finance roads, water, and energy projects.[124] In Nigeria, the local government has been an active participant in both the domestic and international bond markets stimulating the Nigerian capital markets. FGN bonds dominate the bond market accounting for over N4 trillion of the market capitalization of about N5.64 trillion while the addition of Nigeria's sovereign

121 Infrastructure or project bonds are typically issued to support the operations phase of the project's life cycle. During this phase, the bonds are substantially de-risked and operations cash flows are more certain and allow the project to meet its debt service. *See* Strategic Infrastructure, *supra* note 3 at 27.

122 Strategic Infrastructure, *supra* note 3 at 28.

123 *Id.*

124 Harley Tega Williams, Joseph M. Okonkwo & Olaleye Ronke Abolore, The Impacts of Financing Public Utility within a Developing Economy (A Co-Integration Approach) Bonds, Global Journal of Management and Business Research Finance, Vol. 14(1)(2014), *available at* https://globaljournals.org/GJMBR_Volume14/1-The-Impacts-of-Financing.pdf.

bonds to the JP Morgan Government Bond Index—Emerging Markets (GBI-EM) and Barclay's Bank Emerging Markets—Local Currency Index (EM-LCI) has made sovereign bonds more attractive to global investors financing power, gas, transportation, energy, water, sanitation, and communication infrastructure projects.[125] While these instruments can play a vital role in contributing to economic growth, it is important that bond issuance maintains an investment grade rating by "at least one of the major rating agencies such as Fitch, Standard & Poor's and Moody's" thereby enhancing the investor base and creating an active secondary market.[126]

While the majority of third-party funding for PPP projects stems from long-term debt financing, the balance of such funding consists of equity.[127] Typically, equity is utilized during the development and construction strategies of the project cycle where the project contains the most risk.[128] The precise return on equity is dependent on the project's performance post-construction and during operations where there is more certainty on operational and market conditions.[129] However, since the return on equity is only "received after the debt has been serviced, usually later in the life of the project, this higher risk implies higher returns."[130] Projects require equity funding since lenders

125 Financing Nigeria's Infrastructure, *supra* note 14.

126 Strategic Infrastructure, *supra* note 3 at 29.

127 Project Preparation Guide, *supra* note 71 at 27.

128 *Id.*

129 *Id.*

130 *Id.*

mandate a certain "cushion between the cash flow available from the project and that required to service the debt."[131] For this reason, equity has a primary role in helping to absorb the project risk and facilitate funding the debt.[132] According to the Project Preparation Guide, third-party equity investors may be helpful to resolve issues between the other private sector parties. This is important since the return on their investment is dependent on the project contractors' performance.[133]

PPP Projects May Be Funded Through Various Sources

There is no one size fits all solution in financing a PPP project. Given the current state of our global economy, Africa will likely have to rely on mixed sources to fund PPP projects and close the infrastructure gap.[134] One example of utilizing mixed sources of funding in a PPP project is the Lekki-Epe Expressway in Lagos, Nigeria, in 2010. The Lagos State government provided public funding for this, one of the largest PPP deals in Nigeria. In that transaction, the AfDB contributed US$85 million of a 15-year debt. The largest share of private-sector financing was covered by Standard Bank Plc. This transaction was

---

131 *Id.*

132 *Id.*

133 *Id.*

134 Zuzana Brixiova, Emelly Mutambatsere, Cecile Ambert, and Dominque Etienne, *Closing Africa's Infrastructure Gap: Innovating Financing and Risks*, AfDB Africa Economic Brief (April 2011).

particularly significant because it was the first PPP for a toll road in West Africa.[135]

In a more recent PPP project in Abidjan, Côte d'Ivoire, the government sought to cross a local lagoon and connect one of its populated residential districts with a commercial district. In 2012, Bouygues Group, a large French construction company used the African Finance Corporation (AFC) and other institutions to finance a project resulting in the construction of the Henri Konan Bedie Bridge. Notably the project had been under development as a PPP for 15 years. The AFC notes that one of the key aspects of the transaction was that the government agreed to provide a minimum traffic guarantee and financing for a subsidy element to help make the project bankable. Another key aspect was that the project received a Multilateral Investment Guarantee Agency (MIGA) guarantee from the World Bank. The 30-year concession project, which is scheduled for completion in 2015, is expected to reduce congestion.[136]

In Cape Verde, through the concerted efforts of government, private investors, the local utility, and the AFC, a wind independent power plant was developed. According to the AFC, the wind plant currently provides over 20% of Cape Verde's power generation capacity. To

---

135 Press Release, Nigeria: AfDB Approves US$ 85 Million for Lekki Toll Road Project (June 20, 2008).

136 Press Release, Côte d'Ivoire Wins African Transport Deal of the Year, 2012 (Feb. 14, 2013); see also Description, Henri-Konan-Bedie-Bridge *available at* http://www.africafc.org/What-We-Do/Projects/Henri-Konan-Bedie-Bridge-—Cote-d'Ivoire.aspx.

help guarantee the success of the endeavor, the state utility acted as a co-investor and "off-taker," which means that the power purchase agreement contains a minimum take or pay structure backed by government guarantees.[137]

These PPP projects illustrate the unique financing interplay between the public and private sectors, the mix of financial instruments and how the allocation of financial and operational risks among the parties involved—government, private investors and sponsors, lenders, and other funders—can generate successful PPP projects. Accordingly, given the anticipated volume of infrastructure development in Africa, PPPs and the varying finance structures serve as a unique platform for economic growth on the continent.

VII. PUBLIC-PRIVATE PARTNERSHIP RISK ALLOCATION

The use of PPPs "involves a range of different risks."[138] These risks, as a general matter, are categorized as construction risk, financial risk, performance risk, demand risk, and residual risk. Each of these risks is assessed and measured in accordance to the project's existence in the project life cycle. Construction risk is typically associated with "design problems, building cost overruns, and project delays." Financial risk, is often viewed as being "related to variability in interest rates,

137 Description, Cabelioca Wind Farm Project, *available at* http://www.africafc.org/What-We-Do/Projects/Cabelioca-Wind-Farm-Project.aspx.

138 Ter-Minassian, *supra* note 72 at 11.

exchange rates, and other factors affecting costs to finance." Performance risk, is related to the availability of an asset, and the continuity and quality of service provision. Demand risk is the risk related to "the ongoing need for services" while residual risk is "related to the future market price of an asset".[139] Notwithstanding the growing interest by the public sector in the facilitation of infrastructure projects through PPPs and given these risk characteristics inherent in implementing PPPs, much consideration should be given by private and public sector participants as to the risk associated with entering into such structures. For example, the private sector participant in the PPP structure may consider whether:

- The public sector has a strong planning program and allocation process to make sure that payments can be made when they are due;

- Each phase of the project is procured under separate contracts or combined;

- The investors' have any rights and protections in the event of contract issues;

- Profits may be freely repatriated to investors abroad and whether foreign personnel may be used for the project;

139 *Id.*

- The lenders' have any rights and protections in the event of contract issues;
- Contract disputes may be resolved in a seamless manner and the rights and obligations of the parties are clearly set forth;
- Payments will be taxed under the project and in what manner;
- Government support is available to cover various risks;
- The judiciary maintains its independence in decision-making in the event of disputes;
- Protocols exist for any contract changes;
- Payment mechanisms are set out; and
- Unsolicited proposals are permitted and if so, how they are treated.[140]

[140] *See* these questions in the Project Preparation Guide, *supra* note 71 at 14-15.

The public sector in measuring and managing the risk inherent in pursuing a project under the PPP model should ensure the following:

- The existence of a "rigorous project preparation process";
- The bankability of the project;
- The identification of all legal, business, and regulatory risk associated with the project; and
- Whether the environment is conducive for conducting business.[141]

While risk is a major consideration for investment in PPP projects, investors may view PPP investments as economically beneficial. To attract investors and mitigate risks, different types of risk mitigating instruments, such as partial risks guarantees, government exchange guarantees, currency hedging, first loss guarantees, political risk insurance, debt and equity insurance, viability gap financing, and local currency bonds may be offered.

A significant element of evaluating risk under the PPP delivery model includes understanding how risk is allocated. Getting the risk matrix complete and the risk allocation optimized is the main factor in determining whether a PPP will be successfully executed over the life of

---

141 Strategic Steps, *supra* note 1, at 40-41.

the project. Risk allocation requires dividing or sharing the responsibility for dealing with the consequences of each risk between the parties. The objective, can best be summarized as follows:

> "The objective is to allocate the risk to the party best able to control its occurrence and consequences as well as to the party in the best position to assess information about the likelihood of the risk within the context of what is likely to be commercially acceptable to the private sector. There are only three parties to whom the risks can be allocated: users, investors (the private sector), and taxpayers (through the government). Risk does not disappear through contractual structuring; it is simply mitigated and reallocated among the parties."[142]

Risk transfer as a key component of the PPP project delivery model allows the government to relieve itself of risks that are better managed by the private sector. As part of this risk transfer process, the government should assess the risks, "so that it knows what it has to pay the private sector to assume them." To this end, governments make distinctions between project-specific risk, which reflects variations in outcomes for individual projects or groups of related projects, and "market risk, which reflects underlying economic developments that affect all projects,

---

142 *See* Edward Farquharson, Clemencia Torres de Mastle & E.R. Yescombe. How to Engage with the Private Sector in Public-Private Partnerships in Emerging Markets at 31-52, *available at* http://elibrary.worldbank.org/doi/10.1596/9780821378632_CH04.

is not diversifiable, and therefore has to be properly priced."[143]

Research has demonstrated the following about these risks:

> "Risks associated with design, technology, construction, and operation are typically allocated to the private sector, which is usually more efficient at controlling and managing these risks. Other risks may be better managed by the public sector, such as regulatory, environmental, and foreign exchange. Some risks may be shared, such as the risk inherent in the lack of demand for use of the infrastructure project or change-of-law. This exercise is one of the most important in assessing and developing the bankability of the project."[144]

It is also important to note that a PPP structure includes not only the contractual relationship between the public and private sectors but also the network of contracts between private sector parties, banks, insurance carriers, and others that serve to allocate risk among PPP participants. Figure 6 below summarizes a PPP project structure and how risk can be allocated among the project participants.

---

[143] Ter-Minassian, *supra* note 72 at 13.

[144] Farquharson, de Mastle & Yescombe, *supra* note 142.

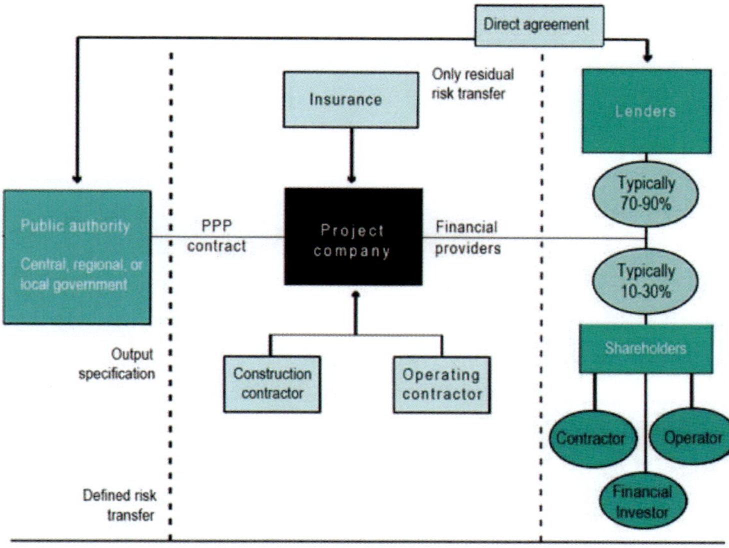

Figure 6
Source: Project Preparation Guide, *supra* note 71 at 28.

VIII. AFRICA PPPS BY COUNTRY

Below is a summary of PPP developments in several African countries where PPP use is growing and PPPs are being used in creative and innovative ways.

a. South Africa

i. Background[145]

South Africa is a middle-income, emerging market with an abundant supply of natural resources; well-developed financial, legal, communications, energy, and transport sectors; and a stock exchange that is the 15th largest in the world. The country possesses modern infrastructure that supports a relatively efficient distribution of goods to major urban centers throughout the region, however, electricity supplies can be unstable. Eskom, the state-run power company, has built two new power stations and installed new power demand management programs to improve power grid reliability. Eskom is also building two new large coal power stations, the completion of which is anticipated between 2015 and 2020. Unemployment, poverty, and inequality remain a challenge, with official unemployment at nearly 25% of the work force. South Africa's economic policy has focused on controlling inflation; however, the country has had significant budget deficits that restrict its ability to deal with pressing economic problems. The current government faces growing pressure from special interest groups to use state-owned enterprises to deliver basic services to low-income areas and to increase job growth. South Africa has increased its use of PPPs in recent years, in part to address these challenges.

---

145 The source of information for each "Background" section is the Central Intelligence Agency, https://www.cia.gov/library/publications/the-world-factbook/ (last visited March 7, 2014).

ii. Regulatory Framework

South Africa remains one of the gold standard countries on the African continent for its national PPP regulatory framework. In April 1997, the South African Cabinet approved the appointment of an inter-departmental task team to develop a package of policy, legislative, and institutional reforms to create an enabling environment for PPPs.[146] By the middle of the 2000s, South Africa had established a PPP Unit in National Treasury,[147] and issued a comprehensive National Treasury PPP Manual designed to outline best practices in every stage of the PPP process,[148] along with Standardised PPP Provisions.[149] Shortly thereafter, the Minister of Finance and Minister for Provincial and Local Government collaborated to issue the Local Government: Municipal Finance Management Act: Municipal Public-Private Partnership Regulations, which govern municipal projects in South Africa.[150]

---

146 Public Private Partnership, Republic of South Africa: National Treasury: PPP Unit, *available at* http://www.ppp.gov.za/Pages/About.aspx (last visited July 23, 2014).

147 *Id.*

148 Public Private Partnership Manual, Republic of South Africa: National Treasury: PPP Unit, National Treasury Practice Note 02 of 2004 through National Treasury Practice Notes 10 of 2004.

149 *Id.* at Practice Note 01 of 2004.

150 *See generally, Municipal Service Delivery and PPP Guidelines of 2007*, National Treasury/Department of Provincial and Local Government (2007) (*available at* http://www.ppp.gov.za/Legal%20Aspects/New%20Municipal%20Service%20Delivery%20and%20PPP%20Guidelines/Municipal

(Footnote continued on next page)

iii. Risks

South Africa is often regarded as one of the easier countries in Africa in which to do business. In 2014, the World Bank ranked South Africa 41st out of 189 countries worldwide for its ease of doing business. Although South Africa received low marks in the category of Getting Electricity (150th), investors should be encouraged by its positive rankings in the categories of Protecting Investors (10th), Paying Taxes (24th), and Getting Credit (28th).[151] Despite favorable economic conditions, there are still some risks associated with PPP investment South Africa. A recent survey of private sector investors in South Africa suggested that the variability of PPP policy in terms of the circumstances in which PPPs are used, changes in political leadership that create an inconsistent commitments to PPP projects, bias toward public procurement, and lack of capacity and experience at the municipal level, all present risks to PPP development in South Africa.[152]

%20Service%20Delivery%20and%20PPP%20Guidelines%20new.pdf) (last visited September 10, 2014).

151 Economy Profile: South Africa at 8-9. World Bank. 2013. Doing Business 2014. Understanding Regulations for Small and Medium-Size Enterprises. Washington D.C., World Bank Group.

152 *Available at* http://castalia-advisors.com/files/12345.pdf. A recent case study illustrates the difficulty in long-term forecasting. In 1999, the Nelspruit Transitional Local Counsel signed a 30-year concession agreement with the Greater Nelspruit Utility Company ("GNUC") to provide water and sanitation services in an underserved region in Northeastern South Africa. The concession was made necessary by a significant change in the boundaries of the region without a similar increase in the amount of funds available for capital investment. At the time, an estimated 45% of the population had no access to water. Under the concession,

(Footnote continued on next page)

iv. Trends In Infrastructure Development

Under South African law, a PPP is defined as "a contract between a public sector institution/municipality and a private party, in which the private party assumes substantial financial, technical, and operational risk in the design, financing, building, and operation of a project."[153] The first PPP projects established in South Africa involved roadways, maximum security prisons, water services, and national parks operation and development. The establishment of the PPP Unit created a central body to oversee and assist PPP projects in a wide variety of sectors.

GNUC was supposed to make the capital investment necessary to provide 24-hour water access to the population, and would be paid by the recipients. However, shortly after the concession was announced, a policy principle was developed in all of South Africa that all indigent households were to receive 6 kiloliters of water per month for free. As a result, people grew reluctant to pay the expected amount for water services, and GNUC became hesitant to make the additional capital expenditures needed to provide 24-hour water access because of its lower than anticipated collections. The contact was renegotiated and the concession continues, but now GNUC receives most of its concession revenue from the state, and GNUC has not made its expected capital contributions at the anticipated level. While overall water access has improved significantly for most of the population, this example illustrates how changing policy and politics can create challenges. Paul Bender and Stewart Gibson, *Case Study for the 10 years of the Mbombela (Nelspruit) Water and Sanitation Concession*, January 2010.

153 Public Private Partnership Manual, Republic of South Africa: National Treasury: PPP Manual Module 1: South African Regulations for PPPs at 4. (available at http://www.ppp.gov.za/Legal%20Aspects/PPP%20Manual/Module%2001.pdf) (last visited October 11, 2014).

The PPP Unit currently consists of seventeen professional staff drawn from both the public and private sectors, with expertise in the following areas: Health, Accommodation, Energy, Education, Water, Budget Support, Transport, Contract Management, Information Communication Technology, Project Development Facility, Tourism, Business Development, Waste, and International Relations.[154]

v. Examples of Current Projects

South Africa has continued to utilize PPP projects in infrastructure development. Key sectors include sanitation, power, and transportation. The following are examples of current projects:

Rolling Stock Fleet Renewal. The Passenger Rail Agency of South Africa recently awarded a contract for 3,600 Electrical Multiple Units and related support and maintenance, worth approximately US$5 billion, to a French based consortium. The project includes the design, manufacture, and maintenance of rolling stock for South Africa's commuter railway passenger fleet. The project will procure the new Electrical Multiple Units over a 20-year period, divided into two ten-year contracts.[155]

---

154 Public Private Partnership, Republic of South Africa: National Treasury: PPP Unit, *available at* http://www.ppp.gov.za/Pages/About.aspx (last visited July 23, 2014).

155 Description, Tender for Rolling Stock Contract via PPP in South Africa (May 1, 2012), *available at* http://infrapppworld.com/2012/05/193.html.

Moloto Corridor Project. The National Department of Transport is finalizing the final valuation of a PPP project for an integrated transport link between Gauteng and Mpumalanga. The project will include rail, road, and transfer facilities and aims to reduce travel time and road accidents on the corridor and provide affordable and safe travel options for commuters. The project will be administered by the Passenger Rail Agency of South Africa. The PPP's funding model is still being finalized. [156]

Department of Transport Fleet Services. A Transport Fleet Services Public Private Partnership was entered into during November 2006 to render vehicle fleet services to six government departments. Services that are provided for in the contract include long-term vehicle rentals, short-term day-to-day vehicle rentals, short medium-term vehicle rentals, a 24-hour Call Centre, chauffeur and point-to-point driver services, an internet based fleet management system with an electronic log book, and a fuel management system.[157]

The Winelands N1/N2 Toll Road Project. In 2011, the South African Roads Agency awarded a PPP contract to the Protea Parkways Consortium. The contract covers upgrading, maintenance, and operation of the N1 and N2 National Routes in the Western Cape as toll roads. The project covers 170km of road and involves building upwards of 170 culverts and bridges, converting a four-lane

[156] Description, Moloto Corridor Project (Aug. 1, 2014), *available at* http://www.engineeringnews.co.za/print-version/moloto-rail-corridor-development-initiative-south-africa-2014-08-01.

[157] Description, Transport Fleet Services

highway into six lanes, building a tunnel through Sir Lowry's pass, and creating overpasses at two points on the N2.[158]

National Parks Projects. South Africa also seeks to develop PPPs for the operation and maintenance of the Castle Rock Caravan Park situated in Sabie; for the design, development, operation, and maintenance of the Graskop Resort in Graskop; and for the operation, development, refurbishment, broad-based black economic empowerment and environmental obligations for the Skukuza airport in the Kruger National Park.

Renewable Energy Independent Power Producer Procurement. In what has been called the most successful public effort to attract private investment in infrastructure in Africa, South Africa has been able to leverage private investment to address key energy needs.[159] The Renewable Energy Independent Power Producer Procurement program is ongoing and, as of May 2014, had already awarded 64 projects to the private sector reflecting US$64 billion of committed investment. Ironically, the project is actually exempt from the PPP regulations because the contracting

---

158 Public Private Partnerships PPP Partnerships Bulletin, South Africa: Winelands N1/N2 Toll Road Project, http://www.partnershipsbulletin.com/projects/view/7264 (last visiting Oct. 11, 2014).

159 D.A. Barber, *Is South Africa A Global Solar-Power Role Model?*, AFKI INSIDER, March 17, 2014, http://afkinsider.com/46910/south-africa-a-global-solar-power-role-model/#sthash.oF9bJ2kY.dpuf.

company is the state-owned power company rather than a state agency. This has given the Renewable Energy Independent Power Producer Procurement program the best of both worlds. It has been able to avoid some bureaucratic hurdles associated with the thorough South Africa PPP process, but also benefitted from the expertise of personnel in the well-established PPP Unit.

b. Nigeria

i. Background

Oil-rich Nigeria has historically struggled with political instability, corruption, inadequate infrastructure, and poor macroeconomic management, but in 2008 began pursuing economic reforms. Nigeria relies heavily on the capital-intensive oil sector, which provides 95% of foreign exchange earnings and about 80% of budgetary revenues. Since 2008 the government has begun to show the political will to implement the market-oriented reforms urged by the international lenders, such as modernizing the banking system, removing subsidies, and resolving regional disputes over the distribution of earnings from the oil industry. GDP rose strongly in 2007–13 because of growth in non-oil sectors and robust global crude oil prices. President Goodluck Jonathan has established an economic team that includes experienced and reputable members and has announced plans to increase transparency, diversify economic growth, and improve fiscal management. Although a lack of infrastructure and slow implementation of reforms are key impediments to growth, the government is working toward developing stronger public-private partnerships for roads, agriculture, and power. Nigeria's financial sector was hurt by the global financial and economic crises, but the Central Bank governor has taken measures to restructure and strengthen the sector including the imposition of mandatory higher minimum capital requirements. Nigeria is a federal system with a centralized national government and 36 states. The three largest states by population include Kano State, Lagos State, and Kaduna State. As noted in the introduction, the Nigerian economy is expected to grow by 7.3% in 2014.

ii. Regulatory Framework

The key legal framework for federal PPPs in Nigeria is provided by the Infrastructure Concession Regulatory Commission Act (2005) and the Public Procurement Act (2007).[160] The Infrastructure Concession Regulatory Commission Act authorizes the granting of PPP projects or concessions, and establishes the Infrastructure Concession Regulatory Commission ("ICRC") to develop the guidelines, policies, and procurement processes.[161] The Public Procurement Act (2007) established the National Council on Public Procurement, which is responsible for montitoring and oversight of PPP projects in Nigeria. Each states has its own procurement and approval processes which are similar to the federal process. Generally an "Office of PPP" or a "PPP Bureau" in each respective state provides the guidelines, policies, and procurement processes, with the State Executive Council being the ultimate approving body.

---

160 *See* Nigeria Public-Private Partnerships Manual, *available at* http://ppptoolkit.icrc.gov.ng/the-enabling-enviroment-for-ppps/the-nigerian-federal-legislative-framework/.

161 Corporate Overview, ICRC, *available at* http://www.icrc.gov.ng/about.php.

iii. Risks

In 2014, the World Bank ranked Nigeria 147th out of 189 countries for its ease of doing business. The relatively low overall ranking was a result of low rankings in the categories of Getting Electricity (185th), Registering Property (185th), Trading Across Borders (170th), Paying Taxes (158th), and Enforcing Contracts (139th).[162] For the most part, however, Nigeria's rankings have remained consistent or improved slightly over the last decade. Other risks to private investment in Nigeria include instability created by various politcal forces, such as geographic and religious divisions. There has also been some internal resistance to PPPs in certain areas. For example, in the last five years, efforts to privatize Nigeria's extensive but aging rail system have been met with opposition from the Nigerian Union of Railway Workers.[163] Moreover, there is disagreement regarding whether Nigeria's Rail Corporation Act (1955) would even permit private ownership or operation.[164] Finally, Nigeria's heavy dependence on oil for its economic growth and stability leave it vulnerable to flucations in oil pricing.

---

162 Economy Profile: Nigeria at 7-9. World Bank. 2013. Doing Business 2014. Understanding Regulations for Small and Medium-Size Enterprises. Washington D.C., World Bank Group.

163 *Nigeria Economy: Faltering Improvements in the Railway System*, Economist Intelligence Unit (Jan. 20, 2014).

164 *Id.*

iv. Trends In Infrastructure Development

The World Bank has been working to develop a regulatory regime in Nigeria that better supports PPP. Although that project is currently being restructured, there are significant PPP opportunities in the pipeline in Nigeria as the federal government and specific governmental regions work to improve infrastructure. At the World Economic Forum, President Jonathon reportedly stated: "We recognize that the private sector will be the engine of growth and job-creation. And we are putting in place the necessary conditions to support this private sector growth."[165] Indeed, Nigeria has developed the Infrastructure Concession Regulatory Commission ("ICRC") with the goal of "accelerat[ing] investment in national infrastructure through private sector funding by assisting the Federal Government of Nigeria and its Ministries, Departments, and Agencies...to implement and establish effective Public Private Partnership's...procurement."

The ICRC is the a federal agency currently responsible for developing or supporting projects in the following areas: Power Generation and Transmission/Distribution Networks; Roads and Bridges; Ports; Railways; Inland Container Depots and Logistics Hubs; Gas and Petroleum Infrastructure such as Storage Depots and Distribution Pipelines; Water Supply, Treatment, and Distribution Systems; Solid Waste

[165] Kehinde, O., 2014. *WEF and the Challenges of PPP in Nigeria, available at*: http://www.thisdaylive.com/articles/wef-and-the-challenges-of-ppp-in-nigeria/178753/ (last visted May 27, 2014).

Management; Educational Facilities (e.g., Schools, Universities); Urban Transport Systems; Housing; and Healthcare Facilities.[166]

In addition, a number of state governments are using PPP to develop infrastructure. Each state is responsible for its own investment projects. However, the federal government does offer some guarantees for state projects.

v. Examples of Current Projects

There are dozens of current PPP projects planned and in progress in Nigeria. Many are transportation projects. For example, in February 2014, the Julius Berger-African Infrastructure Investment Managers, an investment group based in South Africa, was awarded a concession for a US$703 million project involving the construction and development of a 1,590m bridge in Nigeria, known as the Second Niger Bridge (part of the Arterial Route A232).[167] The project is being developed on a design, build, finance, operate, and transfer (DBFOT) basis for a period of 25 years. In addition, prospective developers are competing for a US$450 million project involving the development of the second international airport in Lagos, the Lekki International Airport. That project will be awarded under a

166 ICRC, http://www.icrc.gov.ng/about.php.

167 *Second Niger Bridge PPP Project,* Infra PPP World, *available at* http://infrapppworld.com/pipeline-html/awarded-emea/second-niger-bridge-ppp-project.

Design, Build, Finance, Operate, and Manage (DBFOM) concession agreement.[168]

Many other projects are in social welfare and health care arenas. For example, the Cross River State Government recently sought expressions of interest from developers willing to finance, renovate, operate, and transfer Secondary Health Care Facilities in Bekwarra, Boki, and Obudu under a Public-Private Partnership (PPP) arrangement,[169] and in 2013 awarded a concession to a consortium comprising Utopian Healthcare Consulting, SIMED (the Netherlands), Cure Healthcare Management Services (Hong Kong), CCP (Nigeria), Healthfore (India), and ITB (Nigeria) to construct and operate an 105-bed hospital facility in the Calabar area.[170]

---

168 *Lekki-Epe International Airport Concession,* Infra PPP World, http://infrapppworld.com/pipeline-html/awarded-emea/lekki-epe-international-airport-concession.

169 *Secondary Health Care Facilities in Bekwarra, Boki and Obudu,* Infra PPP World, http://infrapppworld.com/project/secondary-health-care-facilities-in-bekwarra-boki-and-obudu (last visited June 12, 2014)

170 *IFC Helps Nigeria Set Up a PPP For a New 105-Bed Hospital,* International Finance Corporation, http://www.ifc.org/wps/wcm/connect/as_ext_content/what+we+do/advisory+services/about+us/public-private+partnerships/nigeria_crossriverhealthppp (last visited, June 12, 2014).

c. *Ghana*

i. Background

Ghana's economy has been strengthened by a quarter century of relatively sound management, a competitive business environment, and sustained reductions in poverty levels. In late 2010, Ghana was re-categorized as a lower middle-income country. Ghana is well-endowed with natural resources. Agriculture accounts for roughly one-quarter of GDP and employs more than half of the workforce, mainly small landholders. The services sector accounts for 50% of GDP. Gold and cocoa production and individual remittances are major sources of foreign exchange. Oil production at Ghana's offshore Jubilee field began in mid-December 2010, and is producing close to target levels. Additional oil projects are being developed and are expected to come on line in a few years. Estimated oil reserves have jumped to almost 700 million barrels and Ghana's growing oil industry is expected to boost economic growth as the country faces the consequences of two years of loose fiscal policy, high budget and current account deficits, and a depreciating currency. President Mahama has made increasing foreign direct investment a central policy initiative in his administration. However, President Mahama faces challenges in managing a population that is unhappy with living standards and that perceives they are not reaping the benefits of oil production because of political corruption.

ii. Regulatory Framework

Ghana established a National Policy on Public Private Partnerships in 2011 (the "Policy") as a means of leveraging public resources with private sector resources and expertise in order to close the infrastructure gap and deliver efficient public infrastructure and services. The Policy outlines the process for each stage of a PPP project, from development to implementation and evaluation. The Policy outlines the key institutions that will be involved in PPP projects, and provides for the establishment of both a Project and Financial Analysis Unit and a PPP Advisory unit within the Public Investment Division of Ghana's Ministry of Finance and Economic Planning. The Ghana Investment Promotion Center Act of 1994 governs investment in most sectors of the economy.[171] In addition, there are sector-specific laws in areas such as energy and real estate that add sector-specific regulations to the general rules provided by the Ghana Investment Promotion Center Act.[172] Finally, Ghana has also drafted a formal Public Private Partnership bill that is expected to be passed in 2014.[173] The draft bill describes itself as an:

> ACT to facilitate the development and implementation of Public Private Partnership (PPP) projects in Ghana with the view to accelerating the delivery of public infrastructure and related services

---

171 2013 Investment Climate Statement – Ghana, Bureau of Economic and Business Affairs, United States Department of State, *available at* www.stat.gove/e/eb/rls/othr/ics/2013/204648.htm.

172 *Id.*

173 Miguel Martin, Infra PPP World, *Ghana to Approve PPP Law by End of Year*. July 1, 2014, *available at* http://infraworld.com/2014/07/ghana-to-approve-ppp-law-by-year-end.html.

> through partnership arrangements between the public and private sectors, establish institutional structures for the regulation of PPP arrangements, provide the general principles for the identification, structuring, procurement, award, implementation and management of PPPs and to provide for related matters.[174]

Ghana's sustained focus on attracting private investment and facilitating smooth processes for such investment suggests a favorable investment climate for PPP projects.

iii. Risks

In 2014, Ghana was ranked 67th out of 189 countries by the World Bank for ease of doing business. While this is a drop in rank by five spots from its 2013 position, Ghana maintains a significant advantage over it neighbors in sub-Saharan Africa, which have an average ranking of 142. Ghana's relatively positive ranking is driven by strong showings in the area of Getting Credit (28th) and Protecting Investors (34th). However, there is room for improvement in the areas of Dealing with Construction Permits (159th) and Starting a Business (128th). Ghana's economy is expected to have continued strong growth over the next several years due to its investments in the oil and gas sector. However, there are some concerns about inflation (averaging 11.3% in 2014), very low exchange rates for Ghana's currency, the cedi,

174 Ghana Public Private Partnership Bill, Revised Draft Bill – No. 2, May 2013.

and fiscal deficits (expected to be around 9% of GDP in 2014).

iv. Trends In Infrastructure Development

Ghana currently has an infrastructure funding gap of US$1.5 billion and has lagged behind its African peers in attracting outside investment in infrastructure. The President has made increasing foreign direct investment a central policy initiative in his administration. Specifically, there is significant effort being expended in Ghana to create and sustain the institutional capacity for effective PPP arrangements. In addition to the recent PPP Policy and the new proposed legislation, the World Bank is also supporting the launch of PPP projects in Ghana with an US$30 million interest free loan.[175] The loan is intended to provide support in three areas: (1) institutional, financial, legislative, and financial capacity building; (2) PPP pipeline preparation and transaction advisory support; and (3) project management and monitoring and evaluation. The loan is already being used to fund advisory contracts for potential PPP projects in the areas of railway, port, and road transportation.[176]

---

175 Press Release, World Bank, New Partnership Project to Mobilize Private Investment for Ghana's Infrastructure (March 27, 2012), *available at* http://www.worldbank.org/en/news/press-release/2012/03/27/new-partnership-project-to-mobilize-private-investment-for-ghana-infrastructure (last visited Aug. 17, 2014).

176 Miguel Martin, Infra PPP World, *Ghana to Approve PPP Law by End of Year*. July 1, 2014, *available at* http://infraworld.com/2014/07/ghana-to-approve-ppp-law-by-year-end.html.

v. Examples of Current Projects

The opportunities for PPP projects in Ghana span a number of sectors. Planned projects include the Boankra Inland Port and Eastern Railway Line, an office accommodation complex, Winneba College sports and residential/camping facilities, Accra Plains Irrigation, Port of Takoradi improvements, and a Takoradi road dualization project.[177] Although these projects are still in the planning stages—Ghana is seeking transaction advisors to conduct feasibility studies for most of these projects—many are likely to become active PPP opportunities for interested investors. In addition, at least one project has already proceeded to the tender and implementation stage.

Accra Airport Commercial Facility PPP Project. Two public sector entities jointly own a 3.00 acre parcel of land situated within the high value commercial precincts of the Kotoka International Airport. In order to further develop in the region, the government seeks to develop a PPP arrangement with investors to utilize the land for the development of office/mixed-use commercial facility. The PPP was offered on a design, finance, build, operate, maintain, and transfer basis, with the investor transferring the facilities back to the public entities after an agreed period.[178]

177 Infra PPP World, *Projects in Ghana* , available at http://infraworld.com/pipeline-html/projects-in-ghana (last visited July 24, 2014).

178 Infra PPP World, *Tender Launched For Commercial Development At Accra Airport Through* PPP, *available at* http://infrapppworld.com/2013/09/tender-launched-for-

(Footnote continued on next page)

d. Kenya

i. Background

Kenya currently boasts the largest economy in East Africa. However, Kenya's position is threatened by corruption, reliance upon several primary goods whose prices have remained low, and low infrastructure investment. Although the Kenyatta administration has prioritized infrastructure development, international financial lenders and donors remain the key to Kenya's economic growth and development. Unemployment is high at around 40%. The country has experienced chronic budget deficits, inflationary pressures, and sharp currency depreciation—but has recovered following low global food and fuel prices. Recent terrorism in Kenya and the surrounding region threatens Kenya's important tourism industry. Kenya, in conjunction with neighboring Ethiopia and South Sudan, began construction on a transport corridor and oil pipeline into the port of Lamu in 2014.

ii. Regulatory Framework

As part of its efforts to increase private sector investments in infrastructure development, Kenya strengthened its current legal and regulatory framework for carrying out PPPs. In March 2009, the government established an institutional framework under the Public Procurement Disposal Regulations 2009, which help provide operational details on how PPP projects will be prepared and on the roles and responsibilities of the parties

---

commercial-development-at-accra-airport-through-ppp.html (last visited August 28, 2014).

involved in the transactions. Kenya enacted the Public Private Partnership Act, 2013 (Act) which aims to regulate the process of engagement between the private and public parties in order to deliver long-term public goods and provides the scope and type of PPP arrangements. The Act applies to every contract for the financing, construction, operation, equipping, or maintenance of a project. The Act also established a Petition Committee mandated to consider all complaints submitted due to a project agreement and a Facilitation Fund to cover government subsidies, contingent liabilities, and project preparation funds in order to make the projects attractive to the private sector.[179] Under the Act, the Contracting authority must also establish a PPP node,[180] which identifies and screens projects, ensures parties are complying with the act, prepares and appraises each project, and monitors the implementation of the project agreement. After the creation of the node, the contracting authority must meet the PPP Unit, which is the secretariat to the PPP committee in charge of providing advice, educating, making recommendations on projects, and reviewing requests for government support.

179 *Legal & Regulatory Framework of Kenya.* The Public Private Partnership Unit, *available at* http://www.pppunit.go.ke/index.php/legal-regulatory-framework (last visited July 17, 2014).

180 Node is defined as a working group. The key players are the financial officer, technical officer, procurement officer, and legal officer.

iii. Risks

In 2014, Kenya was ranked 129 out of 189 countries by the World Bank for ease of doing business. This is actually a drop in rank by seven spots from the year before. Kenya decreased in all but three of the categories, including Resolving Insolvency (123rd), Getting Electricity (166th), and Registering Property (163rd). Other regulatory issues hurting Kenya's ranking include Paying Taxes (166th) and Trading Across Borders (157th). Kenyan politics will be dominated by the challenges of implementing a new constitution. And while the political violence surrounding the 2007 elections may have subsided, the civil war in neighboring Somalia will continue to be the main source of security- and terrorism-related risk.

iv. Trends In Infrastructure Development

Kenya Vision 2030, a national long-term development blueprint started in 2008, aims to transform Kenya into an industrialized middle income country by 2030. The plan requires heavy investments in infrastructure services. By some estimates, the Kenyan government needs to increase its infrastructure spending to US$4 billion per year, in comparison to its current spending levels of US$1.4 billion. Accordingly, there is plenty of opportunity and need for private infrastructure investment.

v. Examples of Current Projects

The World Bank's International Development Association is supporting Kenya with a US$40 million investment in an Infrastructure Finance Public-Private Partnership Project. In connection with that project, the government and the World Bank have identified pipeline projects, including three that are ready for financing as PPPs, as soon as a PPP framework is in place. These high priority projects are in transport, energy, technology, and trade.[181] The following are examples of PPP opportunities in Kenya:

Kenyatta University Student Housing. Kenyatta University wishes to use a PPP mechanism for procuring and financing the development of housing accommodation for its students. Kenyatta University is a public university, whose main campus is situated on 1100 acres of land, 23 kilometers from the city of Nairobi on the Nairobi-Thika road highway. The Kenyan county of Nairobi began a project in 2013 to build over 80,000 housing units in the Eastlands for resale. The US$500 million project will be handled under PPP framework. It is expected that the construction will take about two years, while operations and transfers may take 10 years. Bidding closed on the project in 2014.[182]

Lake Turkana Wind Power Project. The Project will comprise 365 wind turbines that aim to provide 300MW of reliable, low-cost wind power to the Kenyan national grid, equivalent to approximately 20% of the current installed electricity generating capacity. As of March 2014, this was

---

181 *Private Investors to Raise Stake in Financing Kenya's Infrastructure*. The World Bank, *available at* http://www.worldbank.org/en/news/press-release/2012/11/15/private-investors-raise-stake-financing-kenyas-infrastructure (last visited July 17, 2014)

182 Nduati-Mutero, *supra* note 7.

believed to be the largest wind project in sub-Saharan Africa, and the largest private investment in Kenya's history. The project has been developed by KP&P Africa BV, a group of Dutch entrepreneurs, with Aldwych International as co-developers and Finnfund, IFU, Norfund as investors.[183] The project costs US$842 million and has attracted financial support from the European Investment Bank, Standard Bank of South Africa, East African Development Bank, and African Development Bank. The project is expected to create 2,500 jobs during the 32-month construction period, and 200 full-time jobs during the period of operations. The wind park is expected to be fully commissioned by 2017.[184]

Lamu Port. The aim of the project is to cut over-dependence on Kenya's main port of Mombasa as well as open up Kenya's largely under-developed northern frontier, through creation of a second transport corridor. The project consists of different components including: the Port of Lamu at Manda Bay, a railway line from Lamu to Isiolo, Isiolo to South Sudan, and Isiolo to Ethiopia as well as a highway along the same route.[185] On April 1, 2013,

---

183 *FMO Invests in Lake Turkana Wind Project in Kenya.* FMO Enterpreneurial Development Bank, *available at* https://www.fmo.nl/k/n114/news/view/15126/179/fmo-invests-in-lake-turkana-wind-project-in-kenya.html (last visited July 17, 2014).

184 Description, Lake Turkana Wind Power Project, *available at* http://ltwp.co.ke/.

185 AfDB Keen to Back Lamu Port Project. The Star, Kenya, available at http://www.the-star.co.ke/news/article-21398/afdb-keen-back-lamu-port-project#sthash.Bufwq9fC.dpuf (last visited July 17, 2014).

Kenya's government announced the setting up of a government agency, the Lamu Port Southern Sudan Transport Development Authority that will manage the project on behalf of the Kenyan government. The cost of the project was also put at US$29.24 billion and China Communications Construction Company won the bid to construct the first three berths. The project was developed on a BOT framework and is still ongoing.[186]

Nyali Bridge. The Kenyan government has announced a new plan to construct a second bridge across Mombasa's Tudor Creek in a move to help decongest the island and add a new link to the North Coast currently accessed by the four-lane Nyali Bridge. A Transaction Advisory appointment was made in late 2014 and the project is expected to begin commencement soon.

e. Liberia

i. Background

Liberia is a low-income country that relies heavily on foreign assistance. Although civil war and government mismanagement destroyed much of Liberia's economy, especially the infrastructure in and around the capital, Monrovia, Liberia is in the rebuilding process. Many businesses that fled the country have returned, and with the conclusion of fighting and the installation of a democratically elected government in 2006, the situation is improving. Liberia is richly endowed with water, mineral

[186] Description, Lamu Port, available at http://www.savelamu.org/issues/lamu-port/.

resources, forests, and a climate favorable to agriculture, and iron ore and rubber have driven growth in recent years. Liberia is also reviving its raw timber sector and is encouraging oil exploration. President Johnson-Sirleaf, a Harvard-educated banker and administrator, has taken steps to reduce corruption, build support from international donors, and encourage private investment. Rebuilding infrastructure and raising incomes will depend on financial and technical assistance from donor countries and foreign investment in key sectors, such as infrastructure and power generation. The country achieved high growth during 2010–13 due to favorable world prices for its commodities. In the future, growth will depend on global commodity prices, on sustained foreign aid, trade, investment, and remittances, on the development of infrastructure and institutions, but mostly on maintaining political stability and security.

ii. Regulatory Framework

Liberia has built a strong legal and institutional environment to enable PPPs. Liberia's Contract and Monopolies Commission (CMC), was created in 2003 to oversee contractual agreements undertaken by the National Transitional Government of Liberia (NTGL). The CMC prepared the Interim Public Procurement Policy and Procedures (IPPPP) as well as the Interim Guidelines for Concessions (IGC). The purpose of the IPPPP and IGC was to improve the current public procurement and concessions practices in Liberia by ensuring: competition, economy, efficiency, and transparency. They then became the foundation for the preparation and approval of the Public Procurement and Concessions Act (Act), enacted in 2006. The Act establishes the Public Procurement and

Concessions Commission (PPCC) with oversight responsibility to regulate and monitor all forms of public procurement and concessions practices in Liberia. The PPCC replaced the CMC and regulates all forms of PPPs. The PPCC provides institutional structures for public procurement and concessions, and regulates the methods and procedures for PPP processes.[187]

iii. Risks

In 2014, the World Bank ranked Liberia 144 out of 189 for ease of doing business. This is an improvement from 2013 by five spots. While Liberia has seen an increase in the category of Getting Credit (improving from 105th to 86th), and remained consistent in categories such as Protecting Investors, Liberia ranks low in several categories such as Registering Property (181st), Enforcing Contracts (165th), and Resolving Insolvency (161st). Other challenges to private investments in Liberia include wide spread poverty, unemployment, and illiteracy, and therefore it is difficult to employ laborers. The Democratic system is also fairly new and the country is still stabilizing since the end of the Liberian civil wars. The Ebola outbreak in 2014 has been a major setback to the country's economy. Notwithstanding the current trends, the country's growth rate may be impacted adversely by the results of the Ebola outbreak and poor public infrastructure following the effects of the Liberian civil wars. Moreover, Liberia is very vulnerable to the fluctuation of world oil and food prices.

[187] Brief Background of CMC & PPCC. Government of the Republic of Liberia, available at http://www.ppcc.gov.lr/2content.php?sub=104&related=1&third=104&pg=sp (last visited July 17, 2014).

iv. Trends in Infrastructure Development

The Central Bank of Liberia (CBL) reported a real GDP growth rate of 8.1% for 2013 with inflation averaging 7.6% for the year and has a market-based economy open to foreign investment. Revenues are expected to climb thanks to improved tax administration and export revenues, mainly from the mining sector. At the same time, spending is expected to grow, particularly related to the infrastructure projects (bridges, roads, energy). The budget deficit will be funded by concessional foreign loans, higher customs duties, and, now that the State has re-entered the financial markets, government bond issues.[188]

v. Examples of Current Projects

Liberia's PPP projects have primarily been in the energy, telecommunications, and transportation sectors to encourage economic activity from both foreign and domestic investors. Beginning in 2011, Freeport of Monrovia, Buchanan Port, Greenville Port, and Harper Port became the starting point of a 25-year master plan to aim at revitalizing the post war country's ports to meet international standards. The National Port Authority that developed the Master plan has concessions partnerships with APM Terminals, Firestone, China Union, and Western Cluster. The total capital investment required for implementation is US$2 billion and promises an estimated economic rate return of 21% and an equivalent annual

---

188 *Economic Studies and Country Risks: Liberia.* COFACE, *available at* http://www.coface.com/Economic-Studies-and-Country-Risks/Liberia (last visited July 17, 2014).

return that will be approximately 32% of estimated government revenue.[189]

West Africa Regional Communications Infrastructure Program (WARCIP) Liberia Program. The WARCIP program is a funded organization that aims to increase the geographical reach of broadband networks, reduce the costs of communications services in West Africa, and help regional integration by taking on smaller infrastructure projects. The entire program has an estimated cost of US$56.6 million. For example, Liberia launched the Africa Coast To Europe project[190] under the WARCIP program at a cost of US$25 million. It is still an ongoing project with an expected completion date of September 2015. The public owns 60%, and Libtelco, LoneStar-MTN and Cellcom—all Liberian owned companies—own 20%, 10% and 10% respectively. The lack of access to low price and high quality telecommunications services is one of the factors that presently limit the country's potential to create jobs, expand production of goods and services, and trade competitively with the rest of the world.

---

189 Meeting International Standards: Liberia's National Port Debuts 25 Year Master Plan. The African Standards News, *available at* http://africanstandardnews.org/index.php?option=com_content&view=article&id=1197%3Astaff-report&catid=3%3Anewsflash&Itemid=68 (last visited July 17, 2014).

190 The Africa Coast to Europe (ACE) system is a fiber optic cable system that is run by a consortium led by French Telecom. It will eventually provide broadband connectivity to more than 20 countries. *See* Bonnie Allen and Rob Hugh-Jones, *Liberians Hope Long Wait for the Web is Finally Over,* November 17, 2011, *available at* http://www.bbc.com/news/world-africa-15692430 (last visited Oct. 13, 2014).

The Liberia Electricity Corporation (LEC). The LEC is a Public Corporation solely owned by the Government of Liberia that has a mandate to produce and supply economic and reliable electric power to the entire nation. In April 2010, the International Finance Corporation concluded the tendering of a five-year management contract for LEC, the electricity utility serving Liberia's capital city of Monrovia. Manitoba Hydro International of Canada was awarded the management contract and took over LEC operations on July 1, 2010. At the time LEC had approximately 4,500 connections. A minimum of 33,000 new connections are expected to be set up during the term of the contract, which would result in an additional 150,000 residents of Monrovia having electricity for the first time since the war. The management contract is also expected to result in LEC's improved operational performance over the long term. All investments in transmission and distribution, as well as operator's fees, are being financed by donors. In 2013, IFC structured an amended management contract for LEC. The management contract was extended by 18 months and requires the contractor to connect an additional 75,000 people. The contract accommodated the establishment of a Project Implementation Unit to manage the reconstruction of the 78-megawatt Mount Coffee hydropower plant, an investment estimated at about US$230 million. It is still ongoing.

f. Côte d'Ivoire

i. Background

Côte d'Ivoire is heavily dependent on agriculture and related activities, which engage roughly two-thirds of the population. Côte d'Ivoire is the world's largest producer and exporter of cocoa beans and a significant producer and exporter of coffee and palm oil. Consequently, the economy is highly sensitive to fluctuations in international prices for these products and in climatic conditions. Cocoa, oil, and coffee are the country's top export revenue earners, but the country is also producing gold. The country boasted two off-shore oil finds in 2012. Since the end of the civil war in 2003, political turmoil has continued to damage the economy, resulting in decreased foreign investment and slow economic growth. In June 2012, the IMF and the World Bank announced US$4.4 billion in debt relief for Côte d'Ivoire under the Highly Indebted Poor Countries Initiative.

ii. Regulatory Framework

Côte d'Ivoire does not have a formal PPP law. However, the government has made several recent reforms that promote the development of PPPs in the country. The government has established a National Committee for the Promotion and Development of PPPs. In June 2012, Côte d'Ivoire adopted a new Investment Code to replace the 1995 Investment Code. The new code offers incentives, including tax reductions and exemptions from value-added taxes on equipment for private investors. Under the new code, new industrial zones will be created and investors will benefit from special tax treatment for periods ranging from eight to 15 years, depending on the location of the investment. The new investment code also provides incentives to promote sectors that are essential to the country's economic development, such as low-cost housing construction, the creation of factories, and infrastructure development. In return, investors commit to technology transfer, compliance with environmental regulations, job training, and job promotion. Despite the lack of public-private partnership laws, the environment is still ripe for investment.[191] *Centre de Promotion des Investissements en Côte d'Ivoire* (CEPICI).

iii. Risks

In 2014, the World Bank ranked Côte d'Ivoire 167 out of 189 countries for its ease of doing business. While this is an improvement from last year's rank of 173, the low rank was a result of the following categories: Paying Taxes (173rd), Trading Across Boarders (165th), Dealing with Construction Permits (162nd), and Protecting Investors (157th). While most of the categories remained consistent or decreased slightly from 2013, recent reforms resulted in large jumps in rankings in some categories (e.g., Côte d'Ivoire improved from 179th to 115th in Starting a Business).[192] Another challenge to private investment in

[191] *2013 Investment Climate Statement - Cote d'Ivoire*. U.S. Department of State, *available at* http://www.state.gov/e/eb/rls/othr/ics/2013/204626.htm (last visited July 17, 2014).

[192] *Doing Business 2014*. International Finance Corporation, *available at* http://www.doingbusiness.org/data/exploreeconomies/c%C3%B4te-divoire (last visited July 18, 2014).

Côte d'Ivoire includes electricity. While Côte d'Ivoire is currently working with the IMF to address the electricity pricing structure, it currently is too low relative to the cost of generating it and weighs heavy on the fiscal budget, limiting funds in other sectors.[193] Côte d'Ivoire has potential long-term challenges including political instability and degrading infrastructure. However, there are significant opportunities in Côte d'Ivoire. "Côte d'Ivoire remains one of the largest economies in sub-Saharan Africa and is the largest in Francophone West Africa. It retains an infrastructure superior to most other countries in the region and has been a business and transportation hub since the early 1960s. Buoyed by economic policy reforms, especially in the vital cocoa sector, Côte d'Ivoire's economy has rebounded sharply since the end of the 2010–2011 post-electoral crisis, posting 9.8% GDP growth in 2012."[194]

iv. Trends In Infrastructure Development

The Ivorian government has identified an estimated US$27billion worth of investment opportunities in 170 projects in energy and mining. Côte d'Ivoire aims to become an energy hub for the region by developing its

193 *Monitoring African Sovereign Risk-2013 Quarter 3*. KPMG International Cooperative, *available at* http://www.kpmg.com/Africa/en/KPMG-in-Africa/Documents/2012-2013%20Country%20Profiles/KPMG_Ivory%20Coast%202013Q3.pdf (last visited July 18, 2014).

194 U.S. & Foreign Commercial Service, U.S. Department of State, 2010, Doing Business in Côte d'Ivoire: 2013 Country Commercial Guide for U.S. Companies at 2 (2010).

energy infrastructure, including hydroelectric and solar. The country is also seeking investment in oil and gas, particularly to build a distribution pipeline that can supply the region.[195] A US$120 million, 5-year bond launched by Côte d'Ivoire in August 2012 to raise funds for infrastructure projects was oversubscribed by 46%. The Ivoirian Government, working with the IMF and the World Bank, has taken a number of steps to encourage a more transparent and competitive economic environment. Among these steps are: the creation of a centralized Office of Public Bids in the Ministry of Finance in an effort to ensure compliance with international bidding practices; the use of external financial advisors to work with the privatization committee; the establishment of an inspector general's office for the Government; the dissolution of the non-transparent cocoa and coffee marketing board; and the creation of regulatory bodies for the increasingly-liberalized telecommunications and electricity sectors.[196] In addition, the Public Private Infrastructure Advisory Facility is assisting the Ministry of the City and Urban Public Health in the development of a PPP strategy for solid waste management.

---

[195] Investment Climate Update: Côte d'Ivoire. U.S. Chamber of Commerce, *available at* https://www.uschamber.com/sites/default/files/legacy/international/africa/files/Cote%20d'Ivoire%20ICU.pdf (last visited July 18, 2014)

[196] *Investment Guide*. The Africa-Asia Business Forum, available at http://www.aabf.org/cote_divoire_inv_guide.htm (last visited July 18, 2014)

v. Examples of Current Projects

In its strategic plan 2013–2030 for the development of the electricity sector in Côte d'Ivoire, the Government identified 66 projects that will require massive investment from the private sector, including through PPPs with Independent Power Producers ("IPP"), to expand power capacity production and to modernize the transport and distribution of electricity throughout.[197] Côte d'Ivoire intends to leverage public funds to construct basic infrastructure. Beyond this, the government is seeking private investments to develop road networks, railways, bridges, airfields, and ports.

Henri Konan Bedié Toll Bridge. As noted earlier, the country's first public-private partnership since the civil war involves the financing, design, construction, and operation of the Henri Konan Bedié Toll Bridge and access roads, which indicates the government's willingness to partner with outside investors. The project is a partnership with the Multilateral Investment Guarantee Agency, the political risk insurance arm of the World Bank Group, and will be implemented under a 30-year build-operate-transfer concession agreement.[198]

---

197 *New Developments in the Electricity Sector of Côte d'Ivoire.* Lexology, available at http://www.lexology.com/library/detail.aspx?g=be3be5e4-c4c8-44ec-b3db-4bc1a490be6d (last visited July 18, 2014).

198 *Investment Climate Update:* Côte d'Ivoire. U.S. Chamber of Commerce, available at https://www.uschamber.com/sites/default/files/legacy/international/africa/files/Cote%20d'Ivoire%20ICU.pdf (last visited July 18, 2014)

Abidjan and San Pedro Harbors. Côte d'Ivoire has launched massive upgrades to its ports to support the growth of the natural resource sector and to attract more of the regional transit trade. Côte d'Ivoire has implemented large-scale investments in the transport sector by upgrading its two international harbors: Abidjan and San Pedro. The plans will enable the ports to handle 2.25m twenty-foot equivalent units, making them the ports with the largest capacity in West Africa. In December 2013, the Ivorian authorities and Bolloré Africa Logistics signed a public-private partnership deal, paving the way for the construction of a second container terminal. The Abidjan harbor is the site of a US$2.5 billion expansion project, due to be completed in 2020. According to the government, investment in the San Pedro project will amount to as much as US$825 million.

g. Cape Verde

i. Background

Cape Verde is a small country consisting of a series of islands. Cape Verde has limited natural resources and agriculture. However, Cape Verde's economy has been growing steadily since the late 90s due to its booming service industry. Cape Verde has significant cooperation with Portugal at every level of economy including its currency. While it has minerals, the mining industry is an insignificant contributor to the country's economy. Since 2012, the economy has been hit by the weak international economic situation. GDP growth dropped from 4% in 2011 to 2.5% in 2012 and to 1% in 2013. In order to reduce the budget deficit and curb the high indebtedness trend, the government is shifting the focus from accelerated capital accumulation to improvements in the quality and efficiency of public infrastructure. As a result of the increase in the public sector's borrowing requirements to finance large investments in infrastructure, the total nominal government debt has increased from 69% of GDP in 2009 to an estimated 93% in 2013. Going forward Cape Verde is seeking strategies that can position the country at higher-value stages of the global value chains by stimulating new exports of goods and services and expanding existing ones, especially around the creative sector.

ii. Regulatory Framework

In 2012, Cape Verde enacted a new Investment Code Law (Law 13/VIII/2012). The new Code replaced two previous laws, Law 90/IV/93 of December 13, 1993, and Regulatory Decree 1/94, of January 3, 1994.[199] This legislation came into force January 2013, upon the introduction of the new Tax Incentives Code, (Law 26/VIII/2003). The Tax Incentives Code contains the general principles, contents, and conditions for the granting of tax benefits. It grants a corporate income tax credit of up to 50% of the eligible investments made in activities such as tourism, tourism promotion, air and sea transportation, renewable energy, and information technology. Under the new Investment Code, new rules on foreign investment will be introduced in Cape Verde, but major legal principles, rights, and guarantees are maintained. The key features of the law include: (1) non-discrimination between domestic

---

199 Constance Johnson, *Cape Verde: New Investment Code*. Library of Congress, *available at.* http://www.loc.gov/lawweb/servlet/lloc_news?disp3_1205403284_text (last visited July 18, 2014).

and foreign investors; (2) protection of private property against seizure, nationalization, or expropriation; (3) free currency conversion and transfer abroad of certain income; and (4) the allowance of accounts in multiple currencies for foreign investors. Even without PPP-specific laws, Cape Verde is still a PPP-friendly environment and many deals may be structured in a PPP framework.[200]

iii. Risks

The World Bank ranked Cape Verde 121st out of 189 countries for ease of doing business. This is up seven spots from the previous year and owes the change to its dramatic reforms for starting a business (from 129th in 2013, to 66th in 2014). But it is also the 189th country for resolving insolvency, which might deter investors if there is little to no chance for recovery. Unlike many of its neighboring countries, Cape Verde is known for being a stable country, with no history of political coups or social conflicts. Despite its recent graduation from the list of the United Nation's Least Developed Countries, the government of Cape Verde continues to face great challenges due to the country's insularity and high vulnerability to exogenous shocks.[201] To mitigate the risks of economic downturns and maintain its lower-middle-income status, the government of Cape Verde has committed to modernizing the country's socio-economic

---

200 *Id.*

201 *Economic Studies and Country Risks: Cape Verde.* COFACE, *available at* http://www.coface.com/Economic-Studies-and-Country-Risks/Cape-Verde (last visited July 18, 2014).

infrastructures and implementing a favorable business environment to attract private sector investment.[202]

iv. Trends In Infrastructure Development

Cape Verde's long history of political and social stability continues to be its biggest asset to boost investors' confidence and facilitate private sector participation. With support from technical and financial partners, the Cape Verdean government has committed to providing for the development of new and existing infrastructure in the electricity, water and sanitation, and transport sectors. Various PPP options are being considered for the implementation of these infrastructures, and the government has already prepared a pipeline of potential PPP projects based on PPP framework activity that could be developed in the next five years.[203]

v. Examples of Current Projects

The government of Cape Verde is seeking to mainstream PPPs in the electricity, water, and sanitation sectors. Although Cape Verde has limited PPP experience, the Cape Verdean company of Cabeólica is one of the best examples of PPPs South-Saharan Africa, according to the International Financial Corporation (IFC), of the World Bank group. Cabeólica, founded in 2009, is a renewable

202 *PPIAF Assistance in the Republic of Cape Verde.* Public-Private Partnership Infrastructure Advisory, *available at* http://www.ppiaf.org/sites/ppiaf.org/files/documents/PPIAF_Assistance_in_Cape_Verde_August_2011.pdf (last visited July 18, 2014).

203 *Id.*

energy company that has built four wind farms in Cape Verde, which produced 61.6 million kilowatts of power in 2012, with an estimated saving on imports of 20 million liters of fueloil and diesel in 2012. Cabeólica has contributed to improving the environment in Cape Verde through production of renewable energy.[204]

h. Senegal

i. Background

Senegal's economy is driven by agriculture and that sector is the primary source of employment for the rural areas. The country's key export industries are phosphate mining, fertilizer production, and commercial fishing. The country is also working on iron ore and oil exploration projects. Senegal relies heavily on donor assistance and foreign direct investment. President Macky Sall, who was elected in March 2012 under a reformist policy agenda, inherited an economy with a weak infrastructure, challenging business environment, and a culture of overspending that still plagued the country in 2013. The IMF completed a non-dispersing, Policy Support Initiative program in December 2010 and approved a new three-year policy support instrument to assist with economic reforms. The economy continues to suffer from unreliable power supplies and rising costs of living, which has led to public protests and high unemployment and has prompted

[204] *Cape Verdean Company Cabeólica Named as One of the Best Public-Private Partnerships in Africa*. MACAHUB, available at http://www.macauhub.com.mo/en/2013/04/08/cape-verdean-company-cabeolica-named-as-one-of-the-best-public-private-partnerships-in-africa/ (last visited July 18, 2014).

migrants to flee Senegal in search of better job opportunities in Europe.

ii. Regulatory Framework

Senegal has had a Build-Operate-and-Transfer Law ("BOT Law") since 2004.[205] The BOT law was enacted to set up an appropriate environment for private sector involvement in major public infrastructure development, such as highways and airports.[206] On February 10, 2014, the Senegalese parliament adopted the new Public Private Partnership Act ("The Act"). The Act will replace 2004 BOT Law and it enlarges the scope of the Public Private Partnership by encompassing new sectors like agriculture, education, and health. It also aims at making the investment climate more attractive by setting up several incentive measures. Investment agreements are overseen by the country's investment promotion agency, Agence de Promotion des Investissements et des Grands Travaux (APIX). APIX acts as a "one-stop" investment promotion agency and has been able to guide large-scale PPP investments. APIX also provides administrative support for

205 *Loi relative aux contrats de construction-exploitation-transfert d'infastructures*. Government of Senegal, *available at* http://www.investinsenegal.com/IMG/pdf/loi_relative_aux_contrats_de_construction_exploitation_transfert_d_infrastructures.pdf (last visited July 18, 2014).

206 Abdoulaye Barro, *PPP, Infrastructure, and Decentralization: Perspectives for Senegal*. IP3 Tech Company, *available at* http:://www.ip3.org/ip3_site/ppp-infrastructure-and-decentralization-perspectives-for-senegal.html?print=1&tmpl=component#sthash.wbVChY5V.dpuf (last visited July 18, 2014).

the Conseil présidentiel sur l'investissement, a forum for dialogue among private investors, labor unions, technical and financial partners, and the state to encourage business friendly reforms. In addition to the Build Operate Transfer arrangement under the old BOT law, Senegal utilizes both management contracts (used for the takeover of many State-owned hotels) and leasing (used for the privatization of water and the assignment of vehicles testing activity).[207]

iii. Risks

In 2014, The World Bank ranked Senegal as the 178th best country for ease of business out of 189 countries. It dropped by two spots in rank due to a decrease in several of the rankings. Senegal has the lowest rankings in the following: Getting Electricity 182nd, Paying Taxes (182nd), Registering Property (174th), and Enforcing Contracts (167th).[208] Other challenges to public-private partnerships in Senegal include the poverty and regional disparities and the activity and exports are subject to climatic vagaries, irregular electricity supply, and movements in commodity prices, which could affect the efficiency and stall PPP projects. Senegal's national budget has also been an area of concern, with a fiscal deficit of 5.8% of GDP in 2012, but is expected to improve as recent reforms begin to take

---

207 British Embassy Dakar, *Doing Business in Senegal* at 19. *available at* http://www.developingmarkets.com/sites/default/files/FCO%20445%20Doing%20Business%20in%20Senegal%20Print%20lr.pdf. (last visited Oct. 12, 2014).

208 *Doing Business in Senegal*. IFC, *available at* http://www.doingbusiness.org/data/exploreeconomies/senegal/(last visited July 18, 2014).

effect.[209] The budget process is increasingly transparent and accountable to citizens. A new Tax Code has been introduced and tax reforms are being rolled out, which should begin to increase tax revenues and reduce the budget deficit. In principle, a more transparent budget process should lead to a virtuous circle: citizens will become more willing to pay taxes, but also more determined to hold governments accountable for how their taxes are spent.

iv. Trends In Infrastructure Development

Despite its challenges, Senegal has made enormous progress in recent years in developing an ambitious portfolio of PPPs and continues to stand out as a leader in this area. Senegal has been experiencing several recent PPPs due to its social and political stability. The key sectors for projects have involved energy and transport. Successful PPPs under the BOT law include the development of the Kounoune power plant, which is expected to boost the country's generating capacity to the current 700 MW, and the construction of a section of a Dakar-Diamniadio toll road. As described in more detail below, both of these projects are being expanded due to their success.

---

209 *Development Effectiveness Review2013: Senegal.* AfDB, available at http://www.afdb.org/fileadmin/uploads/afdb/Documents/Project-and-Operations/Development_Effectiveness_Review_2013_-_Senegal.pdf (last visited July 18, 2014).

v. Examples of Current Projects

Senegal has had several successful PPPs, in part due to its social and political stability. Its key sectors for projects have involved energy and transport. The AfDB approved loans for four private infrastructure projects in Senegal between July 2009 and December 2010 to include the expansion of the Dakar Container Terminal, Sendou Power Plant, Dakar-Diamniadio Toll Highway, and New Blaise Diagne International Airport. These four projects represent a total investment of US$1.8 billion in the country. The African Development Bank Group provided financing totaling US$252 million and acted as Mandated Lead Arranger on three of these projects, facilitating a further US$444 million of senior debt for other financial institutions. Key PPP projects include the following:

Dakar Container Terminal. Dakar Container Terminal is a key transportation facility where cargo containers are transshipped between different transport vehicles. The objective of the container terminal PPP is to make the overall container terminal more competitive by modernizing equipment, increasing storage capacity, and enhancing trading volumes. Republic of Senegal released an international invitation to tender for a long-term concession relating to the construction and operation of container terminals. As the successful bidder, DP World FZE signed a 25-year Concession Agreement on October 7, 2007. The Concession Agreement covers the first phase extension of the existing container terminal, in which DP World Dakar intends to carry out improvements, rehabilitation, and construct new infrastructures on the site. The cost for the first phase is estimated at US$284 million, of which the equipment (24%), civil works and development (24%), and concession fee (22%) are the most important items. The African Development Bank (AfDB) has been invited to provide 50% of the total debt, on a par with Standard Chartered Bank. The AfDB is proposing to extend a senior loan of US$64.3 million with an 8-year tenor to part-finance the capital expenditure. Benefits of the project include additional employment for local people, economic stimulation, and indirect benefits for third-party businesses such as suppliers and subcontractors.[210]

Sendou Power Plant. In 2012, Senegal finalized a US$600 million energy deal with Korea Electric Power Corp (KEPCO), which includes the development of a 250-megawatts coal-fired power station, which will be operational from 2015. The aim of the project is to double electricity output and halve the cost of energy to Senegal and it is central to the country's development plan. KEPCO has committed to building the plant station in Senegal with funding from the Korea Development Bank.[211]

Dakar-Diamniadio. To help Senegal improve its transport infrastructure and boost its economy, the IFC and the World Bank, in partnership with Senegal's government and Eiffage, a construction and concessions company, created a public-private partnership to build a landmark toll road connecting Dakar to other parts of the country. After

---

210 Case Study, Dakar Container Terminal, *available at* http://www.pidg.org/impact/case-studies/dakar-container-terminal-senegal.

211 *Senegal, KEPCO sign $600 million coal-fired power station deal.* The Korean Times, *available at* http://www.koreatimes.co.kr/www/news/special/2012/05/176_103654.html (last visited July 18, 2014).

its success in completing the initial section of the toll road, Eiffage won the 30-year concession to build, finance, operate, and maintain the second section of toll road.[212] The estimated cost is US$531 million to complete the project.[213]

New Blaise Diagne International Airport. It will serve as a new airport for Dakar, as the old Léopold Sédar Senghor International Airport is becoming too small for future operations and hopes to encourage more business travel. With a US$450 million price tag the construction of the airport was launched in April 2007. Although it should have lasted 30 months, the project has been subject to some delays (at the time of this publication its last projected completion date was November 2014). Financing is provided by the African Development Bank, the French Development Agency, the West African Development Bank, and other banks from South Africa, Canada, and Saudi Arabia. Once completed, Germany's Fraport, will manage the airport, and the Senegalese state will own a 45% stake, with the remaining 55% held by Aeroport

---

212 *See Senegal's Road to Better Transport.* IFC, available at http://www.ifc.org/wps/wcm/connect/region__ext_content/regions/sub-saharan+africa/news/senegal_toll_road (last visited July 18, 2014); Press Release. *Eiffage wins contract for an extension to Senegal's "Autoroute de l'Avenir" motorway*, Feb. 26, 2014, *available at* http://www.eiffage.com/en/home/actualites/dernieres-infos/mainContent/liste-dactualites/eiffage-remporte-le-contrat-de-l.html.

213 Description, Dakar-Diamniadio Toll Road, *available at* http://www.ifc.org/wps/wcm/connect/industry_ext_content/ifc_external_corporate_site/industries/infrastructure/transportation/tp_casestudies/dakar-diamniadio+toll+road%2C+senegal.

International Blaise Diagne SA, a company owned by Senegalese investors. [214]

i. Ethiopia

i. Background

Ethiopia's economy is based on agriculture but the government is pushing to diversify into manufacturing, textiles, and energy generation. Coffee is a major export crop. The agricultural sector suffers from poor cultivation practices and frequent droughts, but recent joint efforts by the Government of Ethiopia and donors have strengthened Ethiopia's agricultural resilience, contributing to a reduction in the number of Ethiopians threatened with starvation. The banking, insurance, telecommunications, and micro-credit industries are restricted to domestic investors, but Ethiopia has attracted significant foreign investment in textiles, leather, commercial agriculture, and manufacturing. Under Ethiopia's constitution, the state owns all land and provides long-term leases to the tenants; land use certificates are now being issued in some areas so that tenants have more recognizable rights to continued occupancy and hence make more concerted efforts to improve their leaseholds. While GDP growth has remained high, per capita income is among the lowest in the world. Ethiopia's economy continues on its state-led Growth and Transformation Plan under the new collective leadership that followed Prime Minister Meles' death in 2012. The

---

[214] *Dakar's new Blaise Diagne International Airport now delayed until Q4 2014.* The African Aviation Tribune, *available at* http://www.theafricanaviationtribune.com/2012/09/senegal-pics-new-blaise-diagne.html (last visited July 18, 2014).

five-year economic plan has achieved high single-digit growth rates through government-led infrastructure expansion and commercial agriculture development. Ethiopia in 2014 will continue construction of its Grand Renaissance Dam on the Nile—a controversial five billion dollar effort to develop electricity for domestic consumption and export.

ii. Regulatory Framework

Ethiopia does not have a specific PPP law. However, there are some laws and several regulations that are designed to facilitate private investment. For example, in 2009, Ethiopia issued the Ethiopian Federal Government Procurement and Property Administration Proclamation No. 649/2009. The proclamation established the Public Procurement and Property Administration Agency to oversee and manage the procurement process, and the conduct of public suppliers. For foreign investors, the Investment Proclamation of 2012 and the Regulations on Investment Incentives and Investment Areas Reserved for Domestic Investors of 2012, combine to create the primary legal framework governing foreign investment.[215] In addition, there are sector-specific laws that may be relevant to particular projects. For example, in 2007, Ethiopia passed the Solid Waste Management Proclamation No. 513/2007, which allows private operators to obtain a permit to engage in the collection, transportation, and use or disposal of waste. Potential PPP participants in Ethiopia need to investigate and understand the patchwork of laws and agencies that may be relevant to each potential project.

---

215 Invest in Ethiopia, Ethiopian Investment Agency (2013).

iii. Risks

From an investment perspective, Ethiopia has both opportunities and challenges. In 2014, Ethiopia was ranked 128th out of 189 countries by the World Bank for ease of doing business. Ethiopia's ranking has declined slightly over the past few years. It receives low marks in the categories of Starting a Business (166th), Trading Across Borders (166th), and Protecting Investors (157th). However, Ethiopia has stronger scores in the categories of Enforcing Contracts (44th) and Dealing with Construction Permits (55th). It is one of the largest markets in Africa, with approximately 84 million people. Although much of the economy is still heavily controlled by the Ethiopian government, and bureaucratic hurdles can make investment difficult, the Ethiopian government is in the process of making structural reforms to address some of these challenges. The recent establishment of the Ethiopian Investment Agency and the proposed sale of many state-owned enterprises to private investors reflect the government's efforts.

iv. Trends In Infrastructure Development

Ethiopia continues to make significant investments in infrastructure. It has spent the equivalent of US$3.6 billion on road construction and development between 2003 and 2013, and the largest portion of the 2013/2014 budget is slated for road construction. Although PPP investment in roads and infrastructure is welcome and needed, bankable project have been difficult to come by. For example, because Ethiopia has few transportation corridors with the volume of traffic needed to support a toll road, DBO road projects have been few and far between.

Instead, most of the PPP projects in Ethiopia take the form of design/build contracts.

v. Examples of Current Projects

Ethiopia has received funding and grants from the World Bank and the African Development Bank to support the development of infrastructure. Key opportunities for investment in Ethiopia include infrastructure, waste management, and power generation. Various agencies within Ethiopia have engaged in PPP projects. The Micro and Small Enterprises Agency has existing PPPs for housing, road pavement, and textile and food processing services. The Ministry of Urban Development and Construction has entered into a PPP for housing delivery and service. The Ministry of Water and Energy has entered PPPs for irrigation development. Other current projects are as follows:

Addis Ababa Waste to Energy Project. The Addis Ababa Water and Sewage Authority and 4R Energy Company, LEM recently came to terms on a waste to energy PPP. The waste to energy project will convert Addis Ababa's waste water sewage into fuel. The project also aims to reduce carbon emission from Addis Ababa's sewage waste water treatment plants and cut the toxic nutrients being washed into the rivers from the currently open landfill sewage located in Akaki, Addis Ababa. [216]

---

[216] Miguel Martin, Infra PPP World, *Ethiopia Signs Waste To Energy PPP Project*. August 29, 2014 (available at http://infrapppworld.com/2014/08/ethiopia-signs-waste-to-energy-ppp-project.html) (last visited September 5, 2014.)

Privatization of Public Enterprises. The Government of Ethiopia is currently selling 100% of the equity in certain publically held enterprises including: Ethiopian Mineral Development Share Company (Addis Ababa), Bahir Dar Textile Share Company (Bahir Dar), Kombolcha Textile Share Company (Kombolcha), Agricultural Mechanization service enterprise (Addis Ababa), Transport Construction Design Share Company (Addis Ababa), Bilito Siraro Farm (Hawasa), Ethiopia Fiber Product Enterprise's Warehouse (Addis Ababa).[217]

j. Tanzania

i. Background

Tanzania is one of the world's poorest economies in terms of per capita income; however, it has achieved high overall growth rates based on gold production and tourism. Tanzania has largely completed its transition to a liberalized market economy, though the government retains a presence in sectors such as telecommunications, banking, energy, and mining. The economy depends on agriculture, which accounts for more than one-quarter of GDP, provides 85% of exports, and employs about 80% of the work force. The World Bank, the IMF, and bilateral donors have provided funds to rehabilitate Tanzania's aging economic infrastructure, including rail and port infrastructure that are important trade links for inland countries. Recent banking reforms have helped increase private-sector growth and investment, and the government

---

[217] 2014 Investment Climate Statement – Ethiopia, U.S. Department of State, Bureau of Economic and Business Affairs, *available at* http://www.state.gov/e/eb/rls/othr/ics/2014/228384.htm.

has increased spending on agriculture to 7% of its budget. The financial sector in Tanzania has expanded in recent years and foreign-owned banks account for about 48% of the banking industry's total assets. Competition among foreign commercial banks has resulted in significant improvements in the efficiency and quality of financial services, though interest rates are still relatively high, reflecting high fraud risk. All land in Tanzania is owned by the government, which can lease land for up to 99 years. Proposed reforms to allow for land ownership, particularly foreign land ownership, remain unpopular. Continued donor assistance and solid macroeconomic policies supported a positive growth rate, despite the world recession. In 2008, Tanzania received the world's largest Millennium Challenge Compact grant, worth US$698 million, and in December 2012 the Millennium Challenge Corporation selected Tanzania for a second Compact. Dar es Salaam used fiscal stimulus and loosened monetary policy to ease the impact of the global recession. GDP growth in 2009–13 was a respectable 6–7% per year due to high gold prices and increased production.

ii. Regulatory Framework

In recent years Tanzania has taken significant steps to facilitate PPP initiatives. The Public Private Partnership (PPP) Policy was issued in 2009, the Public Private Partnership Act passed in 2010, and the PPP Regulations passed in 2011. The new Public Procurement Act (2011) makes specific provision for PPP procurement, for both solicited and unsolicited proposals.[218] According to the Tanzania Investment Centre, "a Finance Unit (FU) has been created within the Ministry of Finance (MoF) to assess, manage[,] and monitor fiscal risk[;] to assess affordability of projects[;] and to appraise value for money from PPPs with a view to recommend PPP projects for approval by Minister of Finance. A Coordination Unit (CU) has been created within the Tanzania Investment Centre (TIC), which reports to the Prime Minister's Office (PMO). The CU is focusing on promotion and coordination of all matters relating to public private partnerships."[219] These regulations and institutions are all relevant to PPP investors.

iii. Risks

In 2014, Tanzania was ranked 145th out of 189 countries by the World Bank for ease of doing business, an approximate drop of 9 spots. Tanzania scores relatively well in the area of Enforcing Contracts (42nd) and Protecting Investors (98th), particularly compared to neighbors in sub-Saharan Africa. This is good news for potential PPP investors. However, lower scores in the areas of Paying Taxes (141st), Registering Property (146th), and Dealing with Construction Permits (177th) bring down Tanzania's overall ranking.

---

218 Tanzania Investment Centre: Public Private Partnerships, *available at* http://www.tic.co.tz/menu/314 (last visited May 27, 2014).

219 *Id.*

iv. Trends In Infrastructure Development

Much of the current development in Tanzania is focused on increasing capacity for the expected increase in traffic related to energy exploration and development in the Indian Ocean. Key sectors for PPP projects in Tanzania include: road, rail, port, airport, power, and agriculture. While Tanzania is open to both foreign and domestic investment, foreign investors that partner or associate with Tanzanian firms are generally provided some preference in the procurement process.

v. Examples of Current Projects

Currently, the Tanzanian government is working to develop a pipeline of potential projects in the areas of energy (hydro, gas, and wind) and transportation. It is also working to develop best practices for the procurement and operation of such projects. Tanzania maintains a list of all current tenders, including PPP opportunities at http://tender.ppra.go.tz. Here are some examples of current projects in the pipeline:

<u>Mwambani Port</u>. Tanzania is hoping to develop a new port at Mwambani Bay, Tanga, to relieve the pressure on the existing Tanga port, which is operating over capacity. The project is available on a design build and finance basis. The proposed new port is expected to be linked to Lake Victoria by a new rail to be constructed from Tanga to Musoma. The new project will serve both the economy of Tanzania, and the neighboring landlocked countries of Uganda, Rwanda, Burundi, DRC, and southern

Sudan.[220] The project is also being developed on a design, build, and financing basis.[221]

Additional Berths at the Mtwara Port. Tanzania hopes to add four additional berths to the Mtwara Port through a PPP project developed on a design, build, and financing basis. Currently, the port can handle approximately 400,000 metric tons of cargo annually. The goal is to increase annual capacity to 28 million tons by the year 2030. However, traffic is expected to increase with the development of the Mtwara Corridor and energy exploration in the Indian Ocean.[222]

Rail Network. The World Bank's Board of Executive Directors recently approved US$300 million in funds from the International Development Association (IDA) to support the Government of Tanzania's effort to create a reliable open access railway infrastructure on the Dar es Salaam-Isaka section of the East African Central Corridor and to strengthen the country's rail agencies'

220 DIPLOMAT EAST AFRICA,Tanzania Ports Authority: TPA Offers More Routes to EAC. May 6, 2014, *available at* http://www.diplomateastafrica.com/special-reports/tanzania-special-reports/1480-tanzania-ports-authority-tpa-offers-more-routes-to-eac (last visited Oct. 12, 2014).

221 Description, Mwambami Economic Corrider, *available at* http://www.mwaporc.com/.

222 Description, Mtwara Port projects, *available at* http://www.tanzaniaports.com/index.php?option=com_content&view=article&id=131&Itemid=290.

ability to manage the infrastructure, the traffic operations, and the network regulation.[223]

k. Uganda

i. Background

Uganda has substantial natural resources, including fertile soils, regular rainfall, small deposits of copper, gold, and other minerals, and recently discovered oil. Uganda has never conducted a national minerals survey. Agriculture is the most important sector of the economy, employing over 80% of the work force. Coffee accounts for the bulk of export revenues. Since 1986, the government - with the support of foreign countries and international agencies - has acted to rehabilitate and stabilize the economy by undertaking currency reform, raising producer prices on export crops, increasing prices of petroleum products, and improving civil service wages. The policy changes are especially aimed at dampening inflation and boosting production and export earnings. Since 1990 economic reforms ushered in an era of solid economic growth based on continued investment in infrastructure, improved incentives for production and exports, lower inflation, better domestic security, and the return of exiled Indian-Ugandan entrepreneurs. The global economic downturn hurt Uganda's exports; however, Uganda's GDP growth has largely recovered due to past reforms and sound management of the downturn. Oil revenues and taxes are

[223] Deodatus Balile, World Bank Railway Funding Aims to Turn Tanzania into Regional Gateway, World Bank, May 12, 2014, http://sabahionline.com/en_GB/articles/hoa/articles/features/2014/05/12/feature-01 (last visited Oct. 12, 2014).

expected to become a larger source of government funding as oil comes on line in the next few years. Instability in South Sudan is a risk for the Ugandan economy because Uganda's main export partner is Sudan, and Uganda is a key destination for Sudanese refugees. Unreliable power, high energy costs, inadequate transportation infrastructure, and corruption inhibit economic development and investor confidence.

ii. Regulatory Framework

In July 2014, Uganda passed the Public Private Partnership Bill 2012 (the PPP Law). The PPP law is straightforward and aims to establish the framework for a successful PPP program. Under the law, processes for procurement, implementation, maintenance, operation, management and monitoring of PPPs from project inception to conclusion are contemplated. [224] The core infrastructure areas under which PPP arrangements may be entered are in the transportation, telecommunications, social infrastructure, water management, energy related facilities, oil and gas pipelines, tourist infrastructure, sports and recreational facilities, mining as well as any strategic industries.[225] The law itself allows for flexibility in PPP structures and promises to give private and public sector participants some comfort in engaging in PPPs in the country. [226] The Uganda government anticipates that the

---

[224] Noah Edwin Mwesigwa & Hellen Nakiryowa, The Public Private Partnerships Bill 2012: An overview, *available at* http://www.iflr1000.com/NewsAndAnalysis/The-Public-Private-Partnerships-Bill-2012-An-overview/Index/924.

[225] *Id.*

[226] *Id.*

PPP Law will apply to design-build-operate projects across many different sectors.

iii. Risks

In 2015, Uganda was ranked 152 out of 189 countries by the World Bank for ease of doing business. Uganda has improved in the areas of Trading Across Borders (163rd) and Resolving Insolvency (126th), particularly compared to neighbors in East Africa. This is good news for potential PPP investors. However, lower scores in the areas of Getting Credit (125th) and Registering Property (120th) bring down Uganda's overall ranking.

iv. Trends In Infrastructure Development

Much of the current development in Uganda is focused on power generation, road networks, irrigation schemes and improvement of health infrastructure. Key sectors for PPP projects in Uganda include energy and transportation.[227]

v. Examples of Current Projects

Uganda maintains a list of some current tenders, including PPP opportunities at http://www.perds.go.ug/ppp/. Here are some examples of current projects in the pipeline:

[227] The State House of Uganda, Infrastructure Development in Roads, Railways and Energy, *available at* http://www.statehouse.go.ug/national-priorities/infrastructure-development-roads-railways-and-energy.

International Airports. According to the Uganda Civil Aviation Authority (CAA) international airports are slated to be constructed in Arua (West Nile), Pakuba in Murchison Falls National Park, Kabaale oil region in Hoima and Kasese in Western Uganda pursuant to a 20-year Aviation Master Plan (2014-2034).[228] The Master Plan is expected to cost about US$400 million including US$200million earmarked for the renovation of Entebbe International Airport.[229] The CAA expects 7.6 million passengers to use the different airport facilities by 2034.[230] Currently, Entebbe Airport handles two million passengers with capacity to land a Boeing 747/400. The four new airports will be developed under PPP arrangements.[231]

Roads. The country has announced plans to build a new road linking its capital to Jinja, an industrial hub in its east.[232] The World Bank's International Finance Corporation (IFC) had been hired as the road project's transaction advisor to help with the tender.[233] The six-lane, (48-mile) road is expected to be Uganda's second toll road.[234]

---

228 Uganda Aviation Plan Needs $400m, East African Business Week, Feb. 1, 2015.

229 *Id.*

230 *Id.*

231 *Id.*

232 Elias Biryabarema, Uganda Plans $1bln Public-Private Partnership Road Tender in 2015, Reuters Africa (Oct. 16, 2014).

233 *Id.*

234 *Id.*

IX. CONCLUSION

Economic growth and prosperity in Africa depends on a modern infrastructure. It also depends on the use of innovative models such as PPPs that will facilitate and drive development. To this end, PPPs have become the widely perceived answer to facilitating Africa's current infrastructure needs, as well as the necessary participation of, and opportunities for, those in the private sector. The utilization of the PPP project delivery model recognizes that the private sector drives economic growth particularly as Africa embarks on its 20-to-30-year development boom. While it is widely believed that the PPP project delivery model is the answer to stimulating economic growth, it is important to note that PPPs are not a "panacea" for development in Africa. Consistent with this view, an African government's inability to properly and adequately resource its projects can set PPP projects up for failure. Such failure may result from ongoing lack of expertise and resources within those government offices to manage the projects from inception to completion and to understand the requirements tied to working with large financial institutions funding the projects.

Efforts are currently underway to help shore up the public-sector's involvement in facilitating successful PPPs. For example, the work of development banks like AfDB, which, under plans like its Private Sector Development Strategy 2013–2017, is working to implement operational priorities for its regional government members. One ultimate objective of these operational priorities is to help governments eliminate the administrative barriers and increase the ease of doing business for private sector participants. As African governments become more organized and adept at managing infrastructure projects, the infusion of private sector investment should continue to flow more easily and increase—helping Africa achieve its key priority of developing infrastructure. This key priority as outlined in the African Union's Strategic Plan, coupled with private sector investment and financing facilitated by PPPs, will narrow the infrastructure gap. With the narrowing of the infrastructure gap, opportunity is created for greater inter and intra Africa trade and job creation while realizing significant economic, social, and environmental benefits.

Printed in Dunstable, United Kingdom

91343453R00069